Praise for *The One-Idea Rule*

Writing matters a lot—at school, at work, and in life. *The One-Idea Rule* is one really great idea that packs a powerful punch for anyone who needs to improve this important skill. Read this book if you want to learn to focus like a laser beam and write with impact. It's the perfect gift for anyone who needs to write but dreads writing. After reading this book, you'll be able to write. Simple as that.

—Bruce Tulgan, Author of *It's Okay to Be the Boss*, and Founder and CEO, RainmakerThinking, Inc.

A simple yet brilliant distillation of how to improve your writing, Mark Rennella's *The One-Idea Rule* can help to uncover the root cause of many struggles and difficulties often faced by writers—and can also enrich their thinking along the way. From coming up with a title to the nitty-gritty of creating a clear sentence, Mark leaves no component of writing unexamined.

—Michael B. Horn, Author of *From Reopen to Reinvent*

The One-Idea Rule demystifies the writing process, guiding emergent authors through a step-by-step approach to crafting powerful prose that connects with their audiences. This jargon-free handbook is filled with practical instruction and lively examples from a wide range of genres. In addition to teaching how to write well, *The One-Idea Rule* can also inspire readers to believe in their own potential to become great writers. This book is essential reading for those with one goal: write better right now.

—Stephanie Doscher, Ed.D., Director, Office of Collaborative Online International Learning, Florida International University, and Coauthor of *Making Global Learning Universal*.

In today's churn of constant communication, *The One-Idea Rule* is a great anchor for practical application and theoretical exploration on the art of clear comms. Dr. Rennella does justice to a field that continues to assume it needs perpetual revolution when all it really needs is to come back to the basics. No clichéd spins here . . . just great guidance for the next generation of writers.

—Mehmed Ali, PhD, Director of Academic Services, Air University

The One-Idea Rule is the rare book about writing instruction that does not ground itself in a deficit model. Rather than ingraining writers with a sense of dread about their knowledge gaps, the author emphasizes that foundations preexist that even novice writers can build upon to develop their craft organically. *The One-Idea Rule* lowers the threshold for writers to actually begin writing, without sacrificing the complexities that accrue when writing tasks increase in sophistication. Highly recommended especially for novice writers.

—Stefan Gunther, PhD, Associate Vice President Faculty Affairs,
University of Maryland Global Campus.
Adding one more endorsement here:

"*The One-Idea Rule* is the perfect illustration of its own thesis: focused, directional, productive. It describes the theoretical rationale, then offers a logical means of moving from point to point rather than being a catch-all of do's and don'ts. Based on years of teaching in the field, Rennella has written that rarest of books, a textbook that holds our interest like a novel. It will hold our students' interest even better.

—John Paul Russo, Chair, Department of Classics,
University of Miami, and Author of *The Future without a Past*

THE
ONE-IDEA
RULE

Also by Mark Rennella

Entrepreneurs, Managers, and Leaders:
What the Airline Industry Can Teach Us About Leadership
(Coauthor)

The Boston Cosmopolitans:
International Travel and American Arts and Letters

THE
ONE-IDEA
RULE

**An Efficient Way to Improve Your
Writing at School and Work**

Mark Rennella, PhD

Matt Holt Books
An Imprint of BenBella Books, Inc.
Dallas, TX

Matt Holt is an imprint of BenBella Books, Inc.
10440 N. Central Expressway
Suite 800
Dallas, TX 75231
benbellabooks.com
Send feedback to feedback@benbellabooks.com

BenBella and *Matt Holt* are federally registered trademarks.

Printed in the United States of America
10 9 8 7 6 5 4 3 2 1

Library of Congress Control Number: 2023001236
ISBN (trade paperback) 9781637743980
ISBN (electronic) 9781637743997

Editing by Katie Dickman
Copyediting by Lydia Choi
Proofreading by Jenny Rosen and Lisa Story
Indexing by WordCo Indexing Services
Text design and composition by Jordan Koluch
Cover design by Brigid Pearson
Printed by Lake Book Manufacturing

To:

My parents, who sustained me,
My sister, who hears me, and
My sons,
who exceed me

Contents

....

Part III
Advanced Concepts: Complex Applications and Implications of the One-Idea Rule
···

Introduction to the One-Idea Rule

....

Anybody can learn to write clearly for assignments at school and work. Nonetheless, writing can be difficult, and for some it's a real burden. Finishing papers and reports can be unwelcome and daunting to those who have accumulated years of bad habits or anxiety about their written work.

While there are many ways to develop good writing habits, I'd like to offer a novel, straightforward approach that's easy to remember *and* easy to apply. It's called the "one-idea rule," and it asserts the following: **every component of a successful piece of writing should express only one idea**. This truth provides a solid foundation for anybody to improve their writing over time. The chapters in this book are designed to help the reader start from the basics of the one-idea rule and move steadily toward its more advanced applications.

The rule may sound simple, but it took a long time for me to articulate it clearly to myself and then to others. I developed it little by little over several years as I was teaching literature, composition, and history to college students.

In the fall of 1989, I became a candidate for a master's degree in English from my hometown school, the University of Miami. The English department put all its MA candidates to work by pairing each of us with a very experienced teacher of composition. We would attend class, help grade papers, and eventually do some teaching of individual classes on our own. I had a great mentor and learned a lot about how to help students gain confidence in tackling assignments like essays and research papers.

But even at that early stage in my teaching career, I started to encounter a problem in my responses to student essays that would return year after year. What I noticed was that a small but persistent percentage of students would return with the same kinds of writing problems over the course of the semester. Most of them were really trying their best, but many of their sentences were confusing, and their grammar was often faulty. I had read their essays closely, provided a lot of clear editing with my felt marker, and reviewed their grammatical problems. I'd met personally with them, too, to respond to their questions in detail. So, why were these students making so little progress? What was going wrong with my advice?

What I learned years later is that these miscues with grammar, syntax (word order), and clarity were "downstream" problems—problems caused by some issues that began long before the final draft of any document. The earlier—and more important—"upstream" issues often touched on a more basic human challenge that has a big impact on writing: **the ability to focus**.

Whenever a paper lacked focus, it was often because the student was discussing too many ideas floating around a broad topic. These kinds of students were often enthusiastic, and many of their ideas could be interesting, but these ideas were incompletely expressed and fought for the reader's attention among the many other thoughts in an essay. Another kind of unfocused composition resulted from writers who weren't interested in what they were writing or who lacked confidence in their writing ability. Instead of showcasing too many promising ideas, these writers often failed to articulate a main idea that was more than a generality. In trying to stretch a bland idea across several paragraphs, these writers often ran out of energy or imagination to explore a topic in a satisfactory way.

It turns out that problems with grammar, syntax, and style—issues like run-on sentences, subject–verb agreement, incomplete clauses, and mixed metaphors—can be the result of trying to express too many ideas *as well as* too few. These troubles can always be flagged with a red pen, but they often return with regularity. They return because correcting these issues can't inspire a writer to answer two important questions effectively:

- What is the one main message I want to convey?
- Do I care about the message?

Writers not only need a clear focus to make their message understandable to the reader, but they also have to care about that message so that they're motivated to do a good job conveying it. If writers answer these two questions in the affirmative, they may find that many of their technical problems will start to fade away. That's mainly because they are paying attention to their work and are invested in its success. The one-idea rule directs people toward addressing those two fundamental questions as a crucial first step in completing a composition, and the implications of the rule can lead to many more discoveries that can make writing a consistently positive and productive activity. While it is true that grammar is important in writing and that grammatical problems often are a symptom of faulty thinking, writers need to find *and believe in* their own voices before they pay close attention to these finer points of composition.

This book is mainly intended for developing writers approximately aged sixteen to twenty-five, but it also accommodates the needs and interests of other readers who may be motivated to find reliable ways to improve their writing. To accomplish this, the book is separated into three sections: basic, intermediate, and advanced material. Chapters one through six are the heart of the book. The final three chapters focus on aspects of writing that can be more complicated but are nonetheless useful for many writers as they tackle more difficult assignments.

Each chapter ends with a summary section called "Review and Apply," which is designed not only as a review but also, more importantly, as a condensed version of each chapter. These condensed versions will help readers get started with each chapter's particular applications of the one-idea rule. If they're read collectively in order, these summary sections can act as a quick overview to the entire book. If readers are eager to apply these writing tips quickly to their own writing assignments, they can familiarize themselves with the one-idea rule using the overview these Review and Apply sections provide.

The kinds of writing we'll be exploring in *The One-Idea Rule* fall into two broad categories often required in educational and professional settings: expository writing (writing that explains or describes something) and argumentative writing (writing that tries to persuade readers or prove something). Many of us must write to explain or describe a variety of complex topics in the course of our education or jobs. Often, we are also asked for our opinion on a topic or our evaluation of a situation. Both expository and argumentative pieces are used in many assignments for school and work (e.g., essays in high school about a novel or a short story, research papers in college on current events or chemistry, and reports on professional topics like last month's sales activities or recent progress in a drug-prevention program).

While having good ideas matters, communicating those ideas clearly may matter even more. Many brilliant people who would be useful to *all* of us for their ability to solve complex problems sometimes cannot communicate their ideas well to others. In these cases, the potential of their abilities remains far from realized. Luckily, writing and communication are always part of school assignments, and students who are alert to the importance of writing for their long-term success can embrace every writing assignment as an opportunity to improve their performance for the length of their career after formal schooling is over.

Overview of the One-Idea Rule

Each chapter in this book is dedicated to showing how the one-idea rule can help you better understand individual components of a document—like titles, headings, sentences, and paragraphs—and think about long-term strategies to improve your writing by focusing on these components. But before we delve into these important details, it may be helpful to get a feeling for how these parts of a written piece work together optimally in accordance with the one-idea rule. That's especially important because by the time you approach finishing your final draft of a piece, there should be some clear alignment between each of these parts as they all *work together* to support the main theme or argument.

Let's look at how these individual parts interact in two kinds of documents, one simple and the other more complex: a listicle and a book.

A listicle is an article (usually online) that takes the form of a list, either in part or in its entirety. Often, the lists are a response to an opportunity (e.g., "Twelve places where you should vacation this winter") or a problem (e.g., "Six ways to beat the heat").

One recent example is titled "5 Steps to Booking a Cheap Flight Online."* The listicle is made up of two sections: the first describes a problem ("Booking a flight can be one of the most stressful parts of travel!"), and the second section (the list) solves the problem. If we break down the article into its major components, we can see how they all are aligned to support the "one idea" in the title.

---

* Matt Kepnes, "5 Steps to Booking a Cheap Flight Online," Nomadic Matt, updated September 28, 2022, accessed January 6, 2022, https://www.nomadicmatt.com/travel-blogs /booking-a-cheap-airfare-online/.

Title	5 Steps to Booking a Cheap Flight Online
	↑
Section 1	<u>Main Topic of Section</u>: "Booking a flight can be one of the most stressful parts of travel!"
	↑
Section 2	<u>Main Topic of Section</u>: Using the example of traveling from New York to Barcelona, you will learn about the five steps to book an international flight online.
	↑
First Paragraph of Section 2	<u>Main Topic of Paragraph</u>: Here are some good websites to look at.
	↑
First Sentence of Section 2	"First, I'll look at deal websites like Scott's Cheap Flights, Holiday Pirates, or The Flight Deal to see if there are any fare sales going on."

Now, let's look at how these individual parts interact in a book called *Holistic Health for Adolescents*,* which is represented in the table below. Start by reading the text at the left of the table from top to bottom.

---

* Nada Milosavljevic, *Holistic Health for Adolescents* (New York: W. W. Norton & Company, 2016).

The title of the book describes or at least strongly suggests *one main idea* that the book is dedicated to demonstrating or explaining.

#4

Each chapter that makes up this book is also dedicated to exploring one main idea.

#3

Each chapter, in turn, is made up of many paragraphs, all similarly focused.

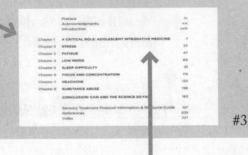

#2

Finally, each paragraph is made up of a collection of sentences, each of which is also dedicated to one idea.

#1

If the writer is keeping a steady eye on developing the main argument or theme set out in the title (in this case, explaining "holistic health for adolescents"), then each part of the book will be related to the others. In this case, the first sentence in Chapter 1 (arrow #1) describes the need to bridge conventional and alternative medicine. The first paragraph where that sentence appears makes a slightly larger and related point (arrow #2) of arguing that holistic medical techniques using the senses can be helpful for adolescents facing many changes in their lives. This idea, then, relates to the theme of the entire chapter (arrow #3), the potential great benefit ("critical role") of applying integrative medicine to help adolescents maintain a positive state of well-being. Finally, this theme is one of eight chapter themes, which, collectively, create an overview of holistic health for adolescents that was set out in the title (arrow #4). These relationships can also cascade downward, from title to sentence (these nuances will be discussed more later).

This pyramid restates the relationships in the holistic-health book example in a more generic way:

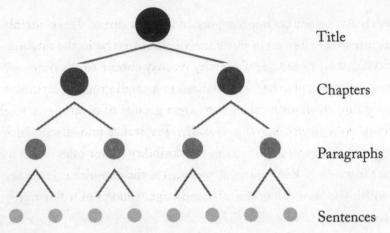

How "The One-Idea Rule" Explains How a Book is Constructed*

These relationships should hold for every well-written piece, from an email to a five-volume history of the Roman Empire. A good way to review how these relationships work is to look at pieces you may read frequently (newspaper articles, novels, blog posts, textbooks) and see how they conform to this architecture. If they don't, then they could probably be improved. As you use the one-idea rule more, you'll be able to recognize when this lack of alignment occurs in the writing of others and, more importantly, in your own.

As you progress through various stages of education and work, the writing assignments you encounter will often become more

---

* This illustration attempts to suggest the ways that all parts of this document hierarchy (title, chapter, paragraph, sentence) can affect one another during the process of writing. During that process, a discovery made while writing a sentence could motivate a writer to modify the title or theme of the entire document. This gives the writer freedom to integrate new discoveries (or ideas) made while writing. It is only toward the final stages of a document that all the writing should strictly conform to the subject or theme suggested in the title.

demanding as well as more important for your career. This is mainly because as we develop in our lives (whether that be in the domains of our careers or in the public roles we may choose to cultivate), we emerge from explaining our opinions to a small group of intimates to sharing them with larger and larger groups of people, many of whom we will not know personally. The stakes and demands of writing grow as we increase the responsibility of our roles—and so can the rewards! Writers can always turn to the one-idea rule as they transition to new responsibilities and larger spheres of influence.

The Rule That Enhances Your Creativity and Keeps You Balanced While Writing

The word "rule" might make people think of restrictions or limits. Often, rules are perceived and used as a way to stop people from doing certain things and looking into new possibilities, or perhaps as a simple means to keep people under control.

But some rules, rightly understood, unlock and enable creativity that otherwise might not be tapped. This can happen in many domains.

Imagine, for instance, that you've received this assignment in an art class: "Draw a picture." The options of responding to this prompt are infinite, but ideas about where to begin are not. That's because creative processes are usually enhanced with parameters that provide something to react or respond to. Those parameters provide some structure—a certain approach to exploring a topic that immediately helps people to see it more clearly because of suggested limits to its scope.

Compare the instruction to "Draw a picture" with these similar assignments that add a rule or two to narrow possibilities but increase the potential for thoughtful responses:

"Using paper and pencil, draw a picture . . .

- . . . that depicts a domestic scene."
- . . . that emphasizes contrasts between light and shadow."
- . . . that looks at the aftermath of a major event (a party, a storm, etc.)."

It turns out that some rules can sharpen your focus. In the above examples, two "rules" concerning an art assignment (i.e., defining a subject and selecting tools to create the art) provide a strong first step for students to become engaged in a topic and start responding with ideas concerning its development. I'm sure you've already thought of some yourself!

For writing assignments, the one-idea rule not only helps to narrow a writer's attention and focus, it can also reliably act as *the first step* in all writing processes.

Before putting down the first word of a document, writers familiar with the one-idea rule will understand how the "micro" parts of a document (sentences, paragraphs) and its "macro" parts (title, theme) are necessarily and vitally related to one another (the focus of part one of this book). They will always know that each sentence they write for any assignment should be oriented toward a theme and that every theme can be either enhanced or modified by a discovery found in a sentence. They'll encounter a true creative tension between these very different parts of the same document, a tension that can sometimes provide a spark summoning unpredictable and creative insights to come forth in the composition process (the focus of part two of this book). *So long as each component is clearly expressing only one idea*, the interplay of the micro and macro elements in a piece of writing can provide rich ground for exploration and development of any topic—like surfing, for example.

Writers can begin small by writing sentences and sentence fragments to find and articulate a theme, as they might during a brainstorming session about the lure of surfing:

- The beauty of the coastline
- The power of waves
- The skills required to successfully balance on a surfboard
- Encounters with fish and birds
- Feeling exhilaration from catching a wave and exhaustion after many attempts
- The community of surfers who share information on surfing, like the best places to surf in the area

Or, if a writer begins with a big idea, that will probably motivate them to create sentences to add appropriate details with examples and explanations:

Idea: "Surfing saved my life: it helped me stop worrying about my future by connecting me so closely to nature in the present."

The basics of surfing, in fact, provide a very apt metaphor for how writers can progress with the one-idea rule. Becoming an expert surfer (like an expert writer) takes years of practice and, especially, learning from trial and error. Nobody can surf really big waves after only a few weeks of lessons. Likewise, no beginning writers will become graceful authors right after reading this book.

But what this book should do is give writers a reliable way to start every writing assignment and improve over time—a way to "pop up" easily, steady their feet, see clearly ahead, and practice with confidence, aiming for bigger goals over time. And, like surfers, all writers will "wipe out" from time to time . . . but that doesn't have to stop them from trying again.

Finally, writers can use the one-idea rule to help them more easily recognize when a sentence and/or paragraph does not belong with a theme and what they can do to transform that incongruence of ideas into an alignment of thought.

Part I

....

Basic Concepts

*Understanding the Principal Components
of Any Document*

Chapter 1

Title/Theme

....

W riting is often compared to a journey, a relatively long process with a beginning, middle, and end that includes a number of uncertainties and surprises along the way. The reason this book on writing begins with the topic of the "Title/Theme" of a document is because a journey usually begins by picking a destination. Even if that destination changes in the middle of the journey, it usually does so only after one has attempted to reach the original destination first. Without envisioning some end point, the "writing journey" becomes rather shapeless. That said, as with any free-thinking traveler, writers can always change directions in the middle of their trip or give up altogether and return home. But for writing to have meaning for the writer and their readers, it eventually has to have a shape or direction that is determined by a theme. That theme can be provisional or exploratory, but it's very helpful in making (and measuring) some progress while writing.

The discussion of titles in this chapter employs essays and stories as the primary examples of writing formats. While titles are important for all kinds of writing, this examination of the impact of titles on the development of a narrative might be most easily depicted in compact format—or in very short stories. But what we learn about titles in the context of stories and essays applies equally to other kinds of writing, which will also be explored in later chapters.

Part I: Think of Your Audience

Writing can seem like a very solitary activity, but it doesn't have to be that way. At its best, writing can feel like a well-imagined exchange with an audience of some sort. Especially for writers who are beginners or unsure of their abilities, imagining a specific audience of some kind (an audience that has a point of view and curiosity about your topic) can be a crucial first step in giving shape and clarity to their writing.

Imagining an audience can be very useful in honing an approach to a subject. The first title created for an assignment can be seen as a thought experiment for a certain kind of person or group. This experiment answers the question "What if I offered a paper for a specific audience with 'Theme A'? And how might the paper change if its subject were treated with 'Theme B' for that same audience?"

While it is true that titles (along with the theme) can always be adjusted as ideas develop in an essay, having some specific approach, some angle, helps to produce work with a clearer focus and, therefore, something more concrete that writers can accept or reject with conviction as they progress in any particular assignment.

I first learned about the benefits of paying close attention to the interests of an audience when I was in fifth grade. This lesson became a vivid part of my memory, and I remember it often when I'm facing obstacles in my work.

On a cool Monday morning in a Miami elementary school called Silver Bluff, my classmates and I were assigned to give a book report in front of our fifth-grade class. My teacher, Mrs. Cervantes, gave us plenty of time and plenty of options to choose from that week. There were probably twenty-five to thirty-five new books displayed in the corner of our schoolroom that day. We could read any one we wanted and then offer a book report, which I hadn't done before.

Unfortunately, I made a big mistake: I waited until the last minute (the day before the report was due) to choose a book. Obviously, time was short, and that required a short book. Luckily, I spied a pretty thin volume made up of mostly pictures: *Looking for Matt, the Cat*. This seemed doable!

On Friday, all the kids were scheduled to give their five-minute book reports. Because my last name began with the letter *R*, many classmates would precede me. The first report was about *Looking for Matt, the Cat*, and so was the second! It hadn't occurred to me that a lot of people would choose one of the shortest books. "By the time my turn comes up," I said to myself, "nobody will want to listen."

Sure enough, every time a student announced that they would be talking about *Looking for Matt, the Cat*, the collective groaning from the audience grew larger. I wished I'd had the time to read another book! I didn't want my classmates to hate my book report, too.

As Anna Peralta was called on by Mrs. Cervantes, I finally

came up with a strategy to entertain the audience. I realized that not only were a third of the reports that day about the same book, but they all were also being told in very much the same way. They simply recounted what happened from page to page and could have all been titled "What Happened to Matt the Cat?" What if I went one step further, taking what happened to Matt and then interpreting its importance for the audience? With this different emphasis, the title of my talk could become "How Did Matt the Cat Feel About What Happened to Him?" I hoped it would work.

When my name was called along with *Looking for Matt, the Cat*, the groans got even bigger. In an attempt to counter this sour mood, I started with my new angle to the book: "How would you feel if you were left alone, were lost, and didn't have anybody to talk to? That's what this cat feels right at the beginning of the story." This new tack on a (now old) story seemed to work. I kept focusing on the different feelings that the story was trying to convey through Matt's journey in an unknown neighborhood (I did this as I moved from picture to picture with the rest of the class). My friends rewarded me with their attention. The presentation ended with a roaring round of applause. The kids *and* I were relieved that my version of the story was not boring—not the same old story told in a familiar way many times before.

Just like I did with my book report, writers and storytellers often adjust the focus of their in-progress work as they imagine their audience's responses. Before I began my book report, my plan had been generally identical to the plans of the other kids who would present before me. I simply benefited from seeing my audience's response to their presentations and making appropriate adjustments to ensure I wouldn't lose their attention. After choosing that different focus, I kept all my interpretations tightly aligned to it (to that "one idea"), which helped to keep the attention of my (often) restless audience.

Part II: Use Titles as Hypotheses About the Best Way to Tell Your Story to an Audience

The process of using a title or theme for a paper as a "work in progress" hypothesis describes the way writers often make adjustments to their themes as they work. When a writer discovers something about a theme that seems uninteresting, confusing, or mistaken, they don't usually abandon or throw away most of the work they've done to that point. Instead, they find a related theme, reassess their arguments and evidence (usually tossing some of those points aside), and then reorder the remaining materials and insights behind a new goal—that new "one idea."

Think of the approach this way: revisions clear the way for better ideas. Most writing starts out with a goal or hunch about what might make for an interesting topic. Reassessing and revising that hunch with an intended audience in mind is a fundamental element in building your writing and thinking toward a better idea. Embracing the revision process does come with an important limitation, however: while a writer is free to explore any topic they choose, once they set a goal, the information following has to be aligned in support of that goal. In short, changing your title is always allowed and to be expected; however, being disciplined *after* you've made that change is a requirement if you want to keep your forward progress *and* your audience's attention.

When I was retelling the story of Matt the Cat to my classmates, I was lucky to be able to judge my audience's interest in real time and amend the theme of my report. I made those changes by deepening the focus on trying to understand the feelings of a lost cat, not just the physical steps of the journey he was taking. Similarly, when you imagine your audience's response to your work in progress, you're trying to figure out what fits and what doesn't in your discussion. But often it's hard to imagine what the audience will think *before* you start to communicate an idea—just as I discovered back in fifth grade.

So, if you need to change course in a written assignment, don't take that as a sign that you're falling short or that you'll never finish up in time. Instead, understand that you're anticipating your audience's response and clearing the way for better ideas—you are getting closer rather than farther away. If you think they won't be interested in the first paragraphs you've created, don't worry! This is just the normal method of trial and error that all experienced writers encounter.

While the final version of a well-written document (like an essay or a research paper) should appear as solid and well shaped as an arrow or a pyramid, the process to get there can be fluid and full of surprises, like finding one's way through a forest. Starting with a title or theme that expresses one clear idea provides the writer with a hypothetical goal or "exit" from that forest. And just as a hiker might try to find his way through unfamiliar territory, an initial title or theme may lead a writer to a dead end or a difficult crossroads. Writers will learn that coming to a dead end is fine; any hypothesis can be incorrect or insufficient. But to find one's way through that forest (or writing assignment), one must eventually learn from mistakes and try another direction.

Eventually, a more fruitful hypothesis can be found that gives the writer a clear direction to emerge from the dark with a completed assignment.

Part III: Exploring the Power of Titles to Shape a Narrative

A collection of ideas, arguments, or facts can be used to support a variety of themes or stories depending on the point of view from which a narrative is told. The classic movie *The Wizard of Oz* features a story told from the point of view of a farm girl from Kansas who dreams of adventures in an amazing fantasy world. Decades later, the Broadway musical *Wicked* took the same basic events from *Oz* and told a very different story from the point of view of the farm girl's nemesis, the Wicked Witch of the West.*

These contrasting stories based on similar materials are successfully told because each maintains a focus on its unique principal theme, which is either suggested or implied by the title (the "one idea" of each performance). While Dorothy and the witch are important in both versions of the history of Oz, only one of these characters decisively shapes each rendition.†

The same can happen for written assignments at school and at

---

* The writer Evan Connell also told two different stories derived from very similar experiences in two novels that look at the life of a married couple, first from the point of view of the wife in *Mrs. Bridge* (1959) and then from that of the husband in *Mr. Bridge* (1969).

† This does not exclude the possibility of telling one story in which both characters are equally important. In this case, the resulting theme would probably be very focused on the rivalry between the two characters. As a result of this equal focus on the two, the feelings aroused by both characters would likely be mixed and complicated for the audience.

work that consider complicated issues. Debates in an MBA class-room or in a courtroom often find advocates of very differing in-terpretations of the same collections of facts. The "winner" of such a debate is usually the side that tells that best story based on the same facts.*

As we will see in the course of this book, writers find that there is a constant back-and-forth between the title/theme of a document and the actual content; each can influence the other. But once the issue of deciding on a theme or title has been settled as the final destination, a writer's productivity (in terms of qual-ity or quantity) can improve markedly by using the title for the alignment of paragraphs and sentences. This alignment makes the storytelling easier and more powerful. In other words, with an ob-jective locked in, writers can "set the compass" and point all their activity (paragraphs and sentences) toward their preferred destina-tion—the "one idea."

Taking an example from a very famous movie, *Star Wars: Epi-sode V—The Empire Strikes Back*, one can appreciate how many dif-ferent kinds of narratives can be derived from the same basic facts of *Empire*, depending on the chosen destination/objective. The movie contains several interesting storylines, but the most important

---

* Because business decisions often require speedy responses to unforeseen internal or ex-ternal circumstances, debates in MBA classrooms often end with more than one probable response to a business problem. The need to respond quickly often means that business leaders have less time than they would prefer to gather information that would help them make a decision. While there may be many possible answers to a business problem, each answer needs to clearly align its facts and arguments behind a particular decision to be persuasive. In law, courts often have strict rules of evidence so as to avoid lawyers creating arguments that have bases in different facts and that therefore cannot be easily compared or evaluated against each other.

theme centers on Luke Skywalker because of the climactic duel between Luke and his father, Darth Vader (aka Anakin Skywalker).

What would happen, however, if the story were told from a very different point of view? From the viewpoint of Luke's sister, Leia, or his friend and rival Han Solo, or even Luke's mischievous robot sidekick, R2-D2? Imagine a story told by one of these characters, create a title, and then see how the ordering of facts to fill and support a story that is *striving toward a clear objective/destination* becomes increasingly clear and easy to create.*

Another way to appreciate the power of titles to shape narrative is to imagine discussions based on a variety of themes about similar recent events. For instance, how many ways can a writer analyze recent trends in TV and movie entertainment in the wake of the COVID-19 pandemic? Based on some preliminary research, I came up with some tentative titles/themes concerning this topic.

---

* I've created an example of the beginning of an alternative story derived from *The Empire Strikes Back* with the character of Yoda as the central figure. The title I chose suggests the difficulty Yoda faces in finding and training a new Jedi who might be able to take on the growing forces of evil in the universe: *"There Is Another": Yoda's Challenge.* Here's the beginning of a story shaped by this alternative "one idea":

- On the planet of Dagobah, Yoda approaches the corner of a swamp where Luke Skywalker has landed. He observes Luke's look of despair and frustration as he surveys his surroundings. Luke talks to himself about Han Solo and Leia.
- In a flashback, Yoda and a younger Obi-Wan Kenobi fight together against evil Jedis. At the end of the fight, they must part but vow to each other to keep working together to bring up a new generation of Jedis.
- Younger Yoda is then seen creating his secretive dwelling in Dagobah. The audience sees his modest dwelling along with his great potential power as he goes through his Jedi exercises.
- The flashback ends. Yoda seems discouraged as Luke demonstrates some impatience and immaturity.
- Etc.

As an exercise, you might want to take up two or three of these titles and see (1) how each title can help to focus your attention and research in a particular way, and (2) how distinct the narratives derived from different titles can become:

- Movie Revolution or Evolution: What Has Changed and What Hasn't Since the Pandemic?
- People Have More Fun Options for Video Entertainment, but Are They Lonelier?
- How Streaming Content and Social Media Have Changed How Movies Are Produced
- In the New World of Cinema, Diversity Wins!

After you've done some research concerning these titles to shape some narratives, you will probably develop some hunches for new themes. See if you can come up with another title of your own and some details that could create the raw material for your own narrative. (This anticipates some of the work you will do during the ideation stage of writing, the topic of chapter four.)

Narratives can benefit from clearly articulated themes and titles in a wide variety of situations. Work emails are an instance of writing that can often be improved from careful use of subject lines (a kind of title). For instance, say that someone needs to contact the finance department to request expedited payment for a contractor's services. Because there are a lot of potential topics to discuss (e.g., money, the contractor, the contractor's paperwork, a time limit), an email's subject line should be broad enough to open the issue, but it shouldn't try to be comprehensive. In this case, effective message titles or subject lines could include:

- Inquiring about late payment for contractor
- Contractor requests expedited payment
- Requesting update concerning invoice #424

Each of these message titles has a clear topic that could effectively serve as the "one idea" concerning this situation.

As with a good title of any document, email subject lines can effectively suggest the breadth or depth of a topic, but they should leave the details to the email body. This is especially true for emails sent to people whom you don't know or who do not work in your organization. Writers of marketing emails are especially aware of this and try their best to entice recipients who are not obliged to open their emails to click through to see their message. The main goal of the well-crafted email subject line is to make the reader want to learn more about some topic (often by using surprises, looming deadlines, and provocations). Some examples include:

- "Our ancestors, the artists" (*surprise* that ancient people might be considered artists on the same level as contemporary artists—for a website on arts and culture)
- "Don't let your rewards points expire" (*looming deadline* to cash in on sales opportunities—for a furniture company)
- "What not to do when hiring a financial advisor" (*provocation* that may instill some worry or fear that the reader is receiving bad financial advice—for a company selling financial products)

Finally, one should always recall that the writer of an email message is crafting a communication that may be forwarded to another recipient; therefore, an important consideration here is to be as direct and as clear as possible. This will help the email message to be focused and on topic, which will lessen the chances of its being misunderstood if it is forwarded to an unexpected audience.

Conclusion: The Potential for Poetry in Titles for Nonfiction Documents

When working on a written assignment for a difficult subject, it's always safe to create a title that tells the reader directly what you're writing about. A paper on DNA in a scientific journal doesn't need a flashy title; the title is there to tell other professionals what they need to know about the information in the paper, such as "A reagent for the single-step simultaneous isolation of RNA, DNA and proteins from cell and tissue samples."* The same goes for papers in social science or business. A paper with a straightforward title like "How supply-chain problems may impact future drug development and distribution" provides a professional audience a perfect preview of the analysis to follow. The ideas contained in the title and subsequent discussion are perfectly aligned.

However, it's often the case that readers know much less about a subject than the writer does. In this case, the writer can create a bridge between their specialized knowledge and the curiosity of the readers: a suggestive or even poetic opening. This connection is usually made in two parts: a title and a subtitle. Typically, the title provides the suggestive language—the "poetry"—to hook the interest of a novice in a subject, and the subtitle provides the focus of

---

* Piotr Chomczynski, "A reagent for the single-step simultaneous isolation of RNA, DNA and proteins from cell and tissue samples,"*Biotechniques* 15, no. 3 (1993): 532–34, 536–37.

the argument, the principal idea that the written piece is exploring. (This enticement of the reader has strong parallels to the subject lines of marketing emails listed above.) In essence, the writer is sharing an overall broad destination of the piece in the title, a place where the expert and the novice can meet.

Here are some examples:

The Digital Classroom: Harnessing Technology for the Future of Learning and Teaching*

"Forest people: The role of African rainforests in human evolution and dispersal"†

"What a Waste: The Unsustainability of Single-Use Plastics and How We Can Do Better"‡

This Great Symbol: Pierre de Coubertin and the Origins of the Modern Olympic Games§

These title–subtitle combinations function like a complex sentence (i.e., a complex "one idea"): the title acts as the dependent clause, and the subtitle acts like an independent clause. By themselves, the subtitles would function as perfectly acceptable titles, but they lack something extra. While they describe the main idea clearly, they don't provide the reader with a motivation to move

---

* Peter John and Steve Wheeler, *The Digital Classroom: Harnessing Technology for the Future of Learning and Teaching* (Abingdon, England: Routledge, 2008).

† Julio Mercader, "Forest people: The role of African rainforests in human evolution and dispersal," *Evolutionary Anthropology: Issues, News, and Reviews* 11, no. 3 (June 2002): 117–24, doi:10.1002/evan.10022.

‡ This is a title of a college research paper that will be discussed in chapter seven.

§ John J. MacAloon, *This Great Symbol: Pierre de Coubertin and the Origins of the Modern Olympic Games* (Chicago: University of Chicago Press, 1981).

more deeply into the argument. Often, titles are an enticement, offering mystery, excitement, or potential insight that connects with reader curiosity.

For writers starting to use this style of titling, beginning with the subtitle is probably the most efficient approach because it is often so firmly connected to the main idea of the written piece. After that connection is established, writers can then more safely experiment with adding more expressive (sometimes poetic) "visions" of the overall message of the paper or book.*

Titles as Strong Sentences with Expressive Verbs

A contrasting but also useful approach to creating nonfiction titles is to use an arresting sentence constructed around an expressive verb. By expressive verb, I mean a verb that also carries some meaning along with it. Writing instructors often advise students to minimize their use of "to have" and "to be" verbs because these verbs act simply as weak connections between a subject and a predicate (e.g., "He was tired," "They have regrets," etc.). Expressive verbs add meaning to subject and predicate beyond a mere connection (e.g., "He struggled to finish the last mile," "They regretted their hasty decision," etc.). A verb that is laden with meaning is the "hook" or bridge that attempts to motivate the reader to learn more.

---

* The title of this book follows this format. The title is straightforward but also expresses a concept that readers are not familiar with, which could arouse the curiosity of readers. The subtitle then explains the essence of the book, which is aimed to offer a relatively easy approach to improving writing that promises some significant benefits.

Here are some examples:

Webb Telescope Embarks on New Era in Astronomy*

Algorithm That Detects Sepsis Cut Deaths by Nearly 20 Percent†

Inflation and Economy Weigh Heavily on Georgia Voters' Minds‡

X-rays Reveal Surprise Van Gogh Self-Portrait§

Since they are generally shorter than the two-part titles discussed above, these one-sentence titles are usually more appropriate for shorter pieces and not as helpful for larger topics covered in long studies or books.

At their best, titles of any kind of nonfiction work condense or summarize the entire work that they introduce. They imply everything from the initial spark of interest or most salient feature of an intellectual journey to its final outcome, the completion of the exploration of a topic (its "one idea"). The "poetry" of these titles suggestively fill in many details without having to name those details explicitly.

---

* "Webb Telescope Embarks on New Era in Astronomy," *Science* 375, no. 6576 (January 2022): 6, doi:10.1126/science.acz9927.

† Sophie Bushwick, "Algorithm That Detects Sepsis Cut Deaths by Nearly 20 Percent," *Scientific American*, August 1, 2022, https://www.scientificamerican.com/article/algorithm-that-detects-sepsis-cut-deaths-by-nearly-20-percent/.

‡ Michael E. Kanell and Greg Bluestein, "Inflation and Economy Weigh Heavily on Georgia Voters' Minds," *Atlanta Journal-Constitution*, July 30, 2002, https://www.ajc.com/politics/inflation-and-economy-weigh-heavily-on-georgia-voters-minds/UXC4K2IYAFBLZERLO2VBBOJ6CI/.

§ Marisa Sloan, "X-rays Reveal Surprise Van Gogh Self-Portrait," *Discover*, August 1, 2022, https://www.discovermagazine.com/the-sciences/x-rays-reveal-surprise-van-gogh-self-portrait.

Review and Apply: Title/Theme

- Choosing a title or theme is like picking a destination to travel to. Writing is the means to get to that destination.

- Before choosing a destination, imagine your audience's interests, abilities, and limitations so that you can best guide them on their journey.

- Think of your theme or title as a hypothesis—a probable answer to a question that might be improved or changed, depending on what you discover while composing.

- While you can change the destination of your writing when you want to, still try to have some destination in mind to avoid writing in circles, going nowhere in particular.

- With your final destination locked in, "set your compass" and align all your activity (paragraphs and sentences) toward that destination—your "one idea."

Chapter 2

Sentences

....

Part I: All the Grammar You Really Need to Know to Get Started

Like any academic area of study, grammar (the technical rules of a particular language) can be very complex. But for the purposes of the one-idea rule, there are two relatively simple points to remember that can help you maintain clarity and focus:

1. Grammatical problems in writing are most visible and important in sentences. Because each sentence should express one complete idea, the grammar used in each sentence needs to be solid so that all the ideas in a document are understood.

2. The most essential grammatical rule pertaining to sentences is that an individual sentence usually succeeds in establishing a clear relationship between two parts of speech: the **subject** and the **predicate**. If a writer can make a clear connection between those two parts of a

sentence, she can then feel confident that the idea being expressed in that sentence is clearly stated. If a writer cannot easily identify those elements of a sentence, then it is time to rewrite.

The subject is the focus of the sentence, sometimes described as the actor:

- **I** see you.
- **The bird** flew toward the lake.
- **She** will be hungry.

The predicate contains a verb and describes what the actor is doing: I **see you.**

- The bird **flew toward the lake.**
- She **will be hungry.**

All of the sentences above are simple sentences, which are characterized as having only one independent clause (a sentence with a subject and a verb) that can stand on its own as a sentence. (There are clauses that can't stand alone as sentences, which are called either dependent clauses or subordinate clauses. These are reviewed later in the chapter.)

Of course, as writers tackle ideas of increasing sophistication, the sentences they use may also become more intricate. An example of this would be: "Although the wind was blowing fiercely from the north, **the bird** was not deterred and **flew** valiantly **toward the lake** where her chicks were nesting." If readers can easily identify the subject and predicate as they're reading a sentence, then that sentence has done its job, no matter how simple or complex the sentence may be. The goal of understanding the basics of a grammatically sound sentence is to make sure that the subject and predicate of a sentence work together to express one idea.

Later in this chapter, we'll review a few of the common and reliable strategies writers can use to add some interesting depth and variations to their work. These strategies will give beginning writers some flexibility as they are working to express new ideas. In addition, we will also review some ways to improve a sentence when its meaning isn't clear.

Becoming comfortable with creating sentences of increasing complexity can take some time and practice. As you are making these changes and experimenting, don't worry that your current abilities are necessarily lacking.

Part II: You're Already Good at the Basics of Grammar, but You Can Always Improve

A fundamental step toward improving one's writing (at any stage of proficiency) is to answer this question: "What kinds of sentences do I feel comfortable creating?" If those sentences are relatively simple, that's fine. Once writers understand their current comfort zone, then they can write mainly within that zone while simultaneously using it as a starting point to stretch their abilities. This way, the development of a writing style can be gradual, memorable, and long-lasting—and more likely to be shaped by an individual writer's worldview and personality.

The sentences we feel comfortable writing should usually end up being grammatically correct because humans are naturally gifted at grammar. As babies turn into toddlers, they start creating a potentially infinite amount of word configurations that result in grammatically intelligible statements. Not only can they create statements according to the rules of grammar, but they also know when some very subtle differences in word choice and word order create statements that are incoherent—that don't make sense grammatically.*

The ability of humans to distinguish between statements that are grammatically sound or unsound even extends to sentences that describe absurd or impossible situations. The linguist Noam Chomsky offers a now well-known example of two sentences that

---

* While a thorough discussion of linguistics is neither appropriate nor possible in this book, I think it's worth quoting generously from Steven Pinker's now classic *The Language Instinct* to make the point about the remarkable grammatical talent all human beings exhibit at very early ages:

> The psychologist Karin Stromswold analyzed sentences containing [auxiliary verbs] from the speech of thirteen preschoolers. The auxiliary system in English (including words like *can, should, must, be, have,* and *do*) is notorious among grammarians for its complexity. There are about twenty-four billion billion [not a typographical mistake] logically possible combinations of auxiliaries (for instance, *He have might eat; He did be eating,* of which only a hundred are grammatical (*He might have eaten; He has been eating*). Stromswold wanted to count how many times children were seduced by several dozen kinds of tempting errors in the auxiliary system—that is, errors that would be natural generalizations of the sentence patterns children heard from their parents . . . For virtually all of these patterns, she found *no* errors among the 66,000 sentences in which they could have occurred.

See Steven Pinker, *The Language Instinct: The New Science of Language and Mind* (New York: HarperCollins, 2007), 272.

describe similarly absurd phenomena, only one of which (the first one) makes sense grammatically:

- Colorless green ideas sleep furiously
- Furiously sleep ideas green colorless*

Examples like these point to a fundamental truth about English: the linchpin of a sentence is the verb. The verb orients the reader and creates the center of gravity for the sentence. It's the lifeline between subject and predicate. If it can't be found or distinguished easily, the "proto-sentence" a writer is attempting to construct (usually in the form of a clause or phrase†) cannot become an intelligible sentence.‡

Regarding grammar, writers should feel confident that they can create grammatically correct sentences because speaking according to the rules of grammar is a natural process of human development.

---

* Noam Chomsky, *Syntactic Structures* (Berlin: Mouton de Gruyter, 1957), 15.

† A phrase is a group of words that often acts like an adjective by modifying a noun of some sort; a clause usually contains a subject and a verb but is not always a complete sentence.

‡ In the above examples, the first sentence makes *grammatical* sense because the reader can identify a word that clearly functions as a verb, which is "sleep." The basic subject and predicate of the sentence is "ideas sleep." In the second sentence, the placement of the word "sleep" directly in front of the noun "ideas" suggests that the word now functions as an adjective (like in the phrases "sleep aid" or "sleep deprivation"). While it could be argued that "green" might function as a verb in the second sentence, the subject it might be attached to is uncertain because that potential noun, "sleep ideas," is modified by an adverb (instead of an adjective). "Furiously sleep ideas" tries to make a phrase by combining noun and verb "ingredients," which is impossible; therefore, the potential verb "green" is not obviously connected to any part of the three-word phrase preceding it.

On this particular issue, there is little debate. Today, the major point of debate about this issue concerns whether grammatically correct language is innate or learned.* But for the purposes of *The One-Idea Rule*, this point is moot. Whatever the origins of language usage by human beings, the outcome is the same: toddlers can communicate with each other and with adults because they all follow shared basic grammatical rules linking subjects and predicates.

As toddlers grow into adults, they don't lose this basic understanding of grammar (as one might infer when they receive reprimands for bad grammar on their written assignments). Grammatical problems often occur when the difficulty of a topic outstrips a person's writing abilities as well as their familiarity with grammatical constructions that difficult ideas sometimes require. These problems also arise when writers don't take the time and effort to express their thoughts *idea by idea* and, instead, rush too quickly through their reasoning or explanations, thus eventually leaving the reader behind them in a flurry of half-realized possibilities.

Despite humans' natural grammatical gifts, it is true that there are some very important and fundamental differences between spoken language and written language. Because of that, writing poses specific challenges that are unique and require special approaches to be addressed. As reviewed in chapter one, imagining an audience before one starts to write helps to bridge the gap between social speaking and solitary writing. While speaking offers lots of instant feedback (from verbal language and body language) concerning the effectiveness of verbal statements—from the most basic ("I want

* For a recent article reviewing the outlines of this debate, see Christian Hejlesen Christensen, "Arguments for and against the Idea of Universal Grammar," *Leviathan: Interdisciplinary Journal in English* 4 (2019): 12–28, doi:10.7146/lev.v0i4.112677.

a banana.") to the most abstract ("Do you solemnly swear to tell the truth, the whole truth, and nothing but the truth, so help you God?")—writing does not offer that feedback.

To bridge the "grammatical gap" between spoken and written language, writers can employ the one-idea rule as a powerful lens that leverages their instinct about spoken language and applies it to evaluating written language. This (unwritten) instinct is that each verbal utterance in a language usually expresses one idea. Applied to written language, if a reader can't clearly understand an idea that a sentence is trying to convey, then that sentence probably needs some changes (sometimes grammatical changes, but not always) to make that idea understandable. Writers can address these problems either by fixing a grammatical issue directly or by restating the idea, often in simpler language than was used originally. The second approach is usually the easiest to pursue.

Let's explore that approach by starting with a particular sentence:

"My friends can be unreliable."

That's a pretty clear and understandable statement. In contrast, if a sentence tries to express more than one idea, it becomes unclear:

"My friends can be unreliable, but I've become an independent person since last year."

Although this sentence is grammatically correct, it is a little confusing. If you're feeling lost after reading that statement, it's because there are two ideas crowding into the space of one sentence. The confusion arises because it is unclear how becoming independent is an outcome of the unreliability of the speaker's friends. There could be many outcomes of said unreliability (one could become angry or frustrated, for instance), but there's no inherent connection between that and one's independence.

Often, the best way to fix a confusing sentence like this one is to follow these steps:

Step 1: Figure out all the ideas trying to be expressed.

IDEA #1	IDEA #2
My friends can be unreliable,	but I've become an independent person since last year.

Step 2: Separate them into individual ideas.

In this particular case, there are two ideas: one focused on the speaker's friends, and the other describing the speaker's growing self-confidence. You'll need to rewrite the sentence so that the two ideas contained in it are expressed completely and separately:

IDEA #1	IDEA #2
My friends can be unreliable,	but I've become an independent person since last year.
(Focus: the speaker's friends)	(Focus: speaker's growing self-confidence)

Step 3: Then, rewrite by expressing each idea with one sentence.

Ideas #1 and #2 are related, but they are different. To rewrite, try to ensure that the two ideas are explained clearly and separately:

IDEA #1	**IDEA #2**
Sentence #1	Sentence #2
(Focus: the speaker's friends)	(Focus: speaker's growing self-confidence)
My friends can be unreliable.	Luckily, I've become a more independent person since last year.

Of course, there are many other ways to rewrite the original sentence that allow the writer to dig more deeply into related ideas that give a fuller explanation of the speaker's state of mind.* But being able to clarify your sentences by using the one-idea rule will help improve your writing as well as clarify your thinking. (In the case of this example, rewriting helps to clarify the relationship between cause and effect in suggesting a reason—growing independence—for the speaker being able to feel less disappointed by his friends' lack of reliability.)

You can practice making sure sentences express only one complete idea each in the following exercise. Below, you will find various attempts at writing clear sentences. For a sentence to be viable, it must discuss only one main idea. These "attempted sentences" will either have too many ideas (more than one) or too few (which usually

---

* "My friends can be unreliable, but I do enjoy being with them. As I've become more independent in the last year, their unreliability has become less of a problem for me."

occurs in an incomplete sentence), or they will successfully focus on only one idea. Try to rewrite the sentences that need correction.

#	Attempted Sentence (Answers in Footnote)*
1	Fly too far.
2	They went to the beach where the sand was hot.
3	The little girl found her lost toy and cried for joy.
4	Motorcycle repair is surprisingly lucrative, and I love comfortable shoes.
5	The beautiful tree, decorated with blooms and surrounded by birds.
6	After finally receiving the food that she had been waiting for all afternoon and thinking about how this opening night meant so much for her, it was a hard time.

Part III: The Utility of Complex and Compound Sentences

These reflections on sentences build directly upon the claim made earlier in this chapter: humans are naturally gifted at grammar. If

---

* 1. Too few ideas; 2. One idea; 3. One idea; 4. Too many ideas; 5. Too few ideas; 6. Too many ideas

we weren't naturally able to place words in an order that followed some rules of grammar, we could not make ourselves understood to one another in verbal exchanges.

But writing clearly in a consistent way does require a challenging progression from spoken language because we don't have interlocutors who can question us when our meaning isn't understood. As writers, we have to imagine those kinds of exchanges, as well as solicit those kinds of exchanges by asking others to react to in-progress drafts. Because writing is usually done alone, I advise those who are unsure about their abilities to create sentences that they feel comfortable writing—sentences that are not too far removed from those they would use regularly in spoken exchanges.*

As a writer becomes more comfortable creating sentences at a certain level of complexity, it will encourage the writer to (1) explore different kinds of sentence structures that allow a wider range of expression, and (2) come up with more probing or sophisticated ideas that demand correspondingly sophisticated sentences. Language (in the form of words and sentences) and ideas have an

---

* It's important to remember that there are definite limits to how conversational your writing can be. While grammar is not a central concern of this book, one should never forget that neglecting attention to grammar creates an almost insurmountable obstacle to describing or explaining ideas (which *is* the central concern of this book). People may be able to ignore grammar in conversation because they can always follow up with questions or read a friend's body language to confirm whether their communication was understood or, at least, seemed to be satisfactory to the person they're talking to. But since most writing is intended for some kind of sphere *outside* of the writer's daily life, one cannot use these supplemental communication signals because the meaning of one's sentences is now almost completely dependent on written words. Bad spelling, sloppy grammar, and the use of slang will guarantee that one's words will not carry their intended meaning and, therefore, that one's ideas will be misunderstood.

ongoing reciprocal relationship: the discovery of new facts or concepts gives rise to new words, and new words can open a person's mind to new concepts (which is one reason why reading is such a valuable activity).

When you feel that simpler sentences no longer effectively convey some of the ideas you are trying to express, you will want to stretch your abilities to incorporate ideas that are more subtle or ambitious. While the paths of more complicated sentences have many variations, we will focus on three easy-to-remember sentence-crafting strategies that should add significant and useful options for writers seeking to add more depth and variety to their work. Above all, remembering the one-idea rule while writing about these more challenging subjects will help you maintain the attention of your readers.

Because Life Can Be Complicated, We Have Complex Sentences

Why people need something, do something, or want something at a certain point in time can be complicated. Actions can be motivated by some longstanding circumstance or moved by a last-minute impulse. Sometimes, individuals are not even sure why they have chosen one path of action over another. Similarly, the world outside of human activity is sometimes extremely complicated; that world is often very difficult to adequately represent or describe without including nuance and complexity.

In other words, there's usually a context (what might also be understood as a reason or a precondition) for almost everything that happens in the world. In writing, the way we often represent the relationship between an action and its context is a complex sentence.

A complex sentence is made up of an independent clause (the main action) and a dependent clause (its reason or context). Clauses, by definition, have both a subject and predicate—in theory, everything you need for a sentence. However, dependent clauses don't make sense by themselves. That is because they focus on providing the context of a main action. They exist to give more meaning to the main action (or the main idea) of a sentence. The complex sentence, then, is a complete thought or idea that tightly binds an action with its context.

For example, consider this dependent clause that provides context concerning why an action is taking place: "because shipping prices have risen." When we read that clause by itself, we find a subject (prices) and a predicate (have risen), but it is an incomplete sentence because it only provides the context for some other unknown main action. When we add the **main action/independent clause,** a complete sentence comes into existence (*complete* because it is a meaningful statement or idea):

- **Coffee is more expensive** now than twelve months ago because shipping prices have risen.
- Because shipping prices have risen, poor **countries encounter difficulties paying** for many basic necessities, like medicine.
- **Inflation is hard to control** because shipping prices have risen.

While all of the bold independent clauses above are meaningful on their own, they are limited in their scope and therefore don't convey much information. Who could be confused by the statement "Inflation is hard to control"? But if readers also know that inflation is becoming difficult to manage *because* of a rise in shipping prices, then they are given much more insight about the reasons why the main action came about. Suddenly, a short clause becomes the center of a much more nuanced, meaningful, and even slightly dramatic complex sentence.*

Books for children rely on simple sentences because their audience's worldview lacks the context that an adult has gained simply through their lived experience. For example, an adult witnessing an awkward exchange at a dinner party might describe that layered moment with the help of complex sentences.

> Janine did not expect to see her ex-husband at the dinner party. When Carl came in through the doorway, she looked at him briefly and then sent an accusing glare across the living room to the host. After a few seconds passed, she quietly put down her drink, took her jacket from the closet, and walked out the door.

A child witnessing the same event might represent it this way: "A lady left the party early. She seemed to be sad."

Of course, simple sentences have the great virtue of conveying information very clearly and can sometimes express absolutely everything you need to say about an idea. And because they are often short, simple sentences can be more easily remembered.

---

* "Because" is a subordinating conjunction. As the description suggests, these conjunctions often introduce subordinate clauses. They often introduce "adverbial" clauses that function like an adverb, adding some detail to describe an action. Other common subordinating conjunctions include the words "although," "before," "when," and "while."

Representing a Strong Relationship Between Two Independent Clauses: The Compound Sentence with Conjunctive Adverbs

In expository and argumentative compositions, writers often need to describe how something works or to explain the reasoning that supports a belief or an opinion. These descriptions and explanations often entail multiple steps that occur in a certain order. The scientific method, for example, is often described as having five sequential stages: ask a question, answer the question with a hypothesis, test the hypothesis with an experiment, collect and analyze data, and then communicate findings.

While each stage of the scientific method is an independent topic, explaining clearly how one stage relates to other stages in the method is very important. This is true for students who are first learning how to answer scientific questions as well as for scientists who need to explain their findings to their peers and to the public.

Conjunctive adverbs can help convey strong relationships between ideas, such as cause and effect ("accordingly"), contrasts ("instead"), and sequence ("finally").

Let's imagine that a scientist and her team have conducted an experiment, and it has failed to produce an anticipated result. In trying to describe the causes or consequences of the failure, the team can use conjunctive adverbs to show connections between that failure and other issues closely related to the experiment. Notice in the following examples that the conjunctive adverb (in bold) connects two independent clauses with the help of a semicolon preceding it and a comma following.

- The experiment failed; **therefore**, we will have to reexamine some of the assumptions we made in our hypothesis. (Cause and effect)
- The experiment failed; **however**, this does not mean that the data we gathered for the experiment was faulty. (Contrasts)
- The experiment failed; **furthermore**, the funding for further research has been temporarily suspended. (Sequence)

The purpose of bringing together two independent clauses in this way is to emphasize that there is a close relationship between them. That relationship, then, becomes the "one idea" represented by two sentences with some important relationship to one another. In grammar, that is called a *compound sentence*.

These strong relationships between ideas soldered together with a conjunctive adverb can be useful in many other kinds of communications:

- Newspapers:
    - The Red Sox traded their star shortstop; of course, this means another disappointment for the team's fan base.
    - The town has announced its plans to build a new high school; in addition, there will be a new principal arriving after construction.
- Public announcements:
    - Repairs to the garage have been delayed for a week; consequently, visitors to the building are encouraged to take the shuttle bus from the remote parking lot.
    - A strong snowstorm will arrive this weekend; therefore, travelers are advised to stay off the roads until Monday.

- Instructions:
  - The use of smartphones of any kind will be prohibited during the test; in addition, no papers or books will be allowed in the auditorium.
  - Keep the device away from heat; likewise, avoid leaving it in the sun for an extended period.

Representing a Weak Relationship Between Two Independent Clauses: The Compound Sentence with Coordinating Conjunctions

Here's another kind of compound sentence that brings together two clauses that are related to one another but have bonds that are not quite as strong as those represented with a conjunctive adverb. These relationships are conveyed with a single comma and a *coordinating conjunction* ("for," "and," "nor," "but," "or," "yet," "so").

- The physicist came to the podium, **and** the audience was excited to hear her theories.
- The data was promising, **but** other scientists had trouble replicating the experiment.
- The sound of the chemical reaction filled the room, **yet** the students remained calm.

The connection between the clauses is clear to the reader, but the writer is not trying to emphasize the importance or necessity of those connections as strongly as with compound sentences that use conjunctive adverbs.

These weak relationships between ideas associated to one

another with a coordinating conjunction can be useful in many kinds of communications:

- Personal notes:
    - Remember to buy some more beer for the Super Bowl party, and don't forget the ice.
    - Pick me up at the airport on time, but don't come too early.
- Reminders/advice:
    - Daylight savings time is coming next Sunday, so don't forget to change the time on your clocks.
    - Try to turn down your thermostat when you leave the house, for energy costs are rising.
- Advertising:
    - Buy in bulk, and you will get big savings!
    - So, you've been exercising, yet you haven't lost weight?

Conclusion: Use Your Understanding of Sentences to Help Repair Confusing Documents

Sentences are the primary vessels of our ideas about the world, and clear sentences are a vital tool to express those ideas in a comprehensible way. If that vessel is carrying too many ideas, it may not reach its destination. If it is carrying too few, it will probably be disappointing.

It's on the sentence level of a document that you can most easily observe how the one-idea rule can make a difference in your writing. When your writing has become confusing, it is likely that some sentences are probably breaking the rule. And if you start off your document with sentences that are confusing or too ambitious, that confusion can spill over to many subsequent paragraphs and then to the rest of the piece you're writing.

To fix writing that seems to have become hard for the reader to understand, look for sentences that need simplifying or clarification. In the exercise discussed earlier in this chapter, we untangled and then articulated individual ideas that were jumbled together in a single sentence. We did this by taking a confusing compound sentence and breaking it down into two simpler sentences, each expressing one idea.

An inversion of this problem occurs when a writer uses too few words to describe an idea. When this happens, those phrases often require a little added detail to understand the writer's intended message. For instance, the example of an incomplete sentence used earlier in this chapter, "fly too far," is an unfinished idea that requires more context to become a meaningful sentence: "Some birds fly too far away from home and don't return safely."

These examples suggest how the one-idea rule can provide a constant measure of the health of your sentences. As you practice with the rule, you'll be able to more easily recognize (and fix) sentences that either say too much or express too little.

Review and Apply: Sentences

- Many ideas do not require complicated sentences to be expressed, but they usually require clear sentences.
- To ensure a sentence is clear, make sure that the subject (or actor) and predicate (or action) are obviously related to each other.

- The verb is the lifeline between the subject and the predicate. Check that the verb in a sentence can be easily found and distinguished by the reader.
- Most confusing sentences try to cover too many ideas at once.
- A confusing sentence can usually be improved either by:
  - Correcting grammatical errors
  or
  - Restating the main idea (or ideas) with words or sentences that are simpler than in the original statement, one sentence per idea.
- Creating better sentences (by either improving their clarity or increasing their complexity) begins with composing at the level of complexity you are already comfortable with.

Chapter 3

Paragraphs

··

Part I: Figuring Out the Uncertain Contours of the Paragraph

At first glance on a written page, paragraphs are easy to identify. They are often made up of two or more sentences grouped together, beginning with an indentation from the left margin or a line break from the preceding paragraph. Then, they usually end with a line that does not quite meet the right margin. Within those irregular borders lies one idea, which is expressed by the collection of sentences within.

Even though paragraphs seem very familiar and easy to understand, they may be the most mysterious parts of any piece of writing. In fact, it may often be hard for a writer to find a reason or iron-clad rule to determine exactly where the main material of one paragraph ends and where the next paragraph should begin. This is also complicated by the question of paragraph readability. Even if a very lengthy paragraph contains sentences that are all relevant to one another, many readers may nonetheless lose interest (or even their place) if a paragraph stretches over too much of a page. But how long is too long a paragraph for a reader? And would a rule of thumb about paragraph length pertain to all potential readers?

Given these uncertainties about the paragraph, how can a writer (especially a beginning writer) feel confident that any particular paragraph has expressed an idea adequately without losing the reader's attention? This challenging task might be accomplished by combining an "objective" rule with the "subjective" judgment of a writer. An approach (or rule) to constructing paragraphs that can help many writers is simply to *start paragraphs with a topic sentence.* This ensures that a well-articulated idea will provide a foundation upon which a coherent paragraph can be constructed. The subjective aspect of delineating a paragraph points to the importance of finding ways to maintain the attention of the reader. A writer may improve paragraph readability by asking herself if the paragraph is too long or if some vocabulary in the paragraph might not be appropriate for a particular audience. The answers to these questions are best determined by the writer's subjective judgment about the audience's needs and preferences—not just the application of an abstract rule.*

There is an exercise you can undertake to see the art and science of paragraphing at work. Look for a written piece online that you can copy and paste into a document of your own. It could be a newspaper editorial, workout routine, or a travel guide of a country or city—any piece that requires several paragraphs to describe or explain something. Combine the paragraphs together from that piece to create one continuous text with no paragraph breaks.

Put it aside for about an hour, and then come back to it and try

---

* See Mike Duncan, "Whatever Happened to the Paragraph?," *College English* 69, no. 5 (May 2007): 470–95.

to determine where paragraph breaks should appear. You'll probably find that some of your paragraph decisions may not correspond to those of the original piece. Your paragraphs may be shorter or longer, or you might have chosen to highlight different aspects of the piece by creating new topic sentences for paragraphs. While your division of the entire text via paragraphs may contribute to some mistakes or confusing messages (which reflects the "objective" or logical aspect of constructing a paragraph), you might also find that the variation of the document you created works perfectly well (which reflects the "subjective" or judgmental aspect of constructing a paragraph). It just might work with a slightly different logic than that of the original (e.g., with longer explanations in longer paragraphs instead of shorter ones).

Part II: Some Approaches to Creating Sturdy Paragraphs

For people who feel unsure about their writing, topic sentences offer a very dependable anchor for creating coherent paragraphs. For instance, if a paragraph opens with the sentence "High school and college students should take advantage of their schools' resources to research career possibilities," then all the sentences in that paragraph should be dedicated to that overarching idea. As you become more experienced, you can retain the utility of a topic sentence (i.e., creating the coherence of a paragraph) without writing a theme out so explicitly—an artful rhetorical maneuver. But for writers without much experience, regularly using opening topic sentences is a perfectly good tool to keep your paragraphs well organized.

Because ideas are often the most potent fuel in writing, it's important that they maintain their energy and power in paragraphs that avoid rambling. This doesn't mean that paragraphs can't be long. If they are created by sentences containing related ideas, paragraphs can be as lengthy as a writer may desire. But writers should strive to make sure that any long paragraph they create is truly the product of sentences that are working together to support one larger, overarching idea.

Well-written paragraphs act as the steps leading to the top of the writing pyramid, which is the title of a paper. These paragraphs accomplish three tasks related to the one-idea rule. First, the paragraphs must all be related somehow to the writer's title or theme. Second, and most importantly, all the sentences in any particular paragraph must "belong" together to ensure that the paragraph is dedicated to one idea. (Often, writers can be careless in adding a sentence that seems interesting but isn't germane or may just repeat the message of a sentence appearing earlier in that paragraph). Third, the length of paragraphs should tend to be relatively modest to avoid slowing down the pace of the composition.

Part III: Transitions and Paragraphs

If, as I claimed in the beginning of this chapter, paragraphs are the most mysterious component of any composition, then making transitions between these strange entities can seem especially challenging. Yet these connections that stitch paragraphs together are crucial to successful writing; otherwise, readers can become disoriented. And if readers encounter too many poor transitions, they are likely to abandon an argument (unless they have to read it for an assignment). In fact, because the parameters of a paragraph are almost intrinsically difficult to determine with certainty (often involving subjective judgment concerning their coherence as well as potential appeal to the reader), we may be led to a very counter-intuitive approach to determining the "borders" of any particular paragraph.

It turns out that successful paragraphs are not defined strictly by the coherence of the content within them. A very long paragraph with internal consistency may nonetheless pose difficulties in transitioning to the subsequent paragraph. That is because the "one idea" of a very long paragraph may become somewhat obscured by many subtly similar ideas used to develop an extended description or argument. *The appropriate length of a paragraph, then, might be determined in large part by the paragraph's ability to facilitate a transition to the subsequent paragraph.*

Clear topic sentences also help to "demystify" paragraphs and provide the conceptual foundations that allow paragraphs to be stitched or hooked to one another. The stronger the foundations of each paragraph, the easier it is to create reliable connections between them. The topic sentence can appear anywhere in the paragraph—at the beginning, middle, or end—depending on the intent and skill of the author.

Transitions are sometimes needed to help writers keep related parts of an argumentative structure in a logical sequence. At other times, they're less necessary to developing the content from the writer's point of view, but they are more needed to keep the attention and focus of the audience. In either case, transitions from paragraph to paragraph perform the very important function of reassuring readers that they will not lose their way in the middle of a document because they can trust the writer is leading them through the document with care.

Let's look at a couple of ways to assess the effectiveness of the paragraph below in terms of its conduciveness to transitioning to the subsequent paragraph:

Lilla Cabot Perry (1848–1933) began her supervised artistic training relatively late in life, when her work would progress significantly. Perry only received her first formal art training at the age of thirty-six in 1884. Apparently self-taught up to that point, the work which she completed on her own before 1884 suggests that she had considerable talent. During the next three years she painted with a series of Boston-based artists who had trained in France—Alfred Quentin Collins (1884), Robert Vonnoh (1885), and Dennis Miller Bunker (1886)—before leaving with her husband to France for what would be a two-year stay.*

In the passage above, the topic sentence is in its most common location: the beginning of the paragraph. The sentence (and the entire paragraph) suggests that a chronological story will follow; accordingly, the first sentence of the subsequent paragraph does move forward chronologically, satisfying reader expectations of a smooth transition: "During this first visit to France, Lilla sufficiently improved her skills at two French painting academies to have two of her works admitted to the *Salon de la Société des Artistes Français* of 1889."

One thing to remember if you're ever worried about making an effective shift from one topic to the next is that you should feel free to make transitions as explicitly as you like. As always, elegance in

---

* Mark Rennella, *The Boston Cosmopolitans: International Travel and American Arts and Letters* (New York: Palgrave Macmillan, 2008), 117.

writing is much less important than clarity. If you need to call out a transition in an obvious way (e.g., "the next step in the oxidation process is . . ."), that is perfectly acceptable because it acts as a helpful guide to the reader.

At the other end of the spectrum is a topic sentence that is implicit (perhaps better described as the "central idea" of a paragraph). For example, the original version of the paragraph about Lilla Cabot Perry did not include the topic sentence in bold. I just added that extra sentence for the purpose of explanation. The topic sentence in the original version was an implied topic sentence and not stated directly; nevertheless, the idea in that topic sentence is central to the content of that paragraph. If you read the paragraph *without* the first sentence in bold, it is still coherent to the reader and supports the implicit main idea.

Conclusion: Using Transitions to Maintain the Reader's Attention

One of the outcomes of making good decisions about paragraphs is keeping the reader's attention. For example, a very long paragraph is not incorrect per se, because it may all be focused on one idea; however, the length of that paragraph can make it challenging for the reader to maintain their attention on the argument within it. That is because a paragraph makes an implicit declaration to the reader that "this is one sustained thought." That thought, no matter how useful or insightful, can tire a reader if it continues for too long. This is especially true for a series of long paragraphs.

A paragraph break implicitly gives permission for the reader to pause at an end point of sorts and think about the argument in that paragraph before moving on. Fewer breaks mean fewer opportunities to slow down and reflect. This permission to pause is similar to a transition in that it helps maintain the reader's attention and their train of thought. Without it, a reader could get lost in the details of a long explanation.

Effective transitions between sentences within a paragraph also function to maintain reader attention. Writers can use many phrases or idioms to signal to the reader that they are either continuing an argument or changing to another one. A good example of a "transition tool" that continues a line of argument is the widely used idiom "in fact." This is a connection between two sentences used to signal to the reader that the second sentence is providing more information about something that was just mentioned. For example, one might follow the sentence "I don't like beer" with this information: "In fact, I don't care for any kind of alcohol." This is just one device among many that tells the reader when a writer is maintaining focus on a particular argument.

There are also devices that signal to the reader that there will be a change in the argument. One "transition tool" to signal this change is the phrase "as I was saying . . . ." This phrase is used at the end of a digression and marks when the writer or speaker is returning to the main argument. For example, a historian discussing the controversy surrounding the presidential campaign of 2000 might allow himself a paragraph or two about the details of a personal meeting with George W. Bush but will then get back to the main point by writing, "As I was saying, the conflict over counting votes in Florida put the country through unusual stress."

In addition to making transitions between and within paragraphs, you can plan the overall ordering of ideas according to some sort of framework. A framework contains an implicit sequence that includes natural transitions that are easy to make (once the framework is in place). These transitions happen both between paragraphs and between sections of a document (if the document requires two or more sections). Frameworks also help to maintain reader attention by letting the reader know that an argument will follow in a predictable and understandable way. This discussion on frameworks will be expanded in chapter five on the topic of composing, which looks at a document in its entirety rather than its constituent components.

Review and Apply: Paragraphs

- Use a topic sentence as the central idea of a paragraph.
- After determining the topic sentence, dedicate all the remaining sentences in that paragraph to the idea conveyed in the topic sentence.
- Opening paragraphs with a clear topic sentence offers a reliable method to create coherent paragraphs.
- In general, keep paragraphs to a modest length to avoid slowing down the pace of a document.
- Consider each paragraph as a stepping stone that directs the reader toward the "final destination" of a document.
- Determine the "health" of a paragraph by checking if it succeeds in its role of taking up the idea from the passages preceding it and also setting the stage for the paragraph that will follow.

Part II

···

Intermediate Concepts

Writing a Paper/Creating a Document

Chapter 4

Ideation

....

Part I: Be an Idea Generator

Have you ever read an article, attended a class, listened to a speech, gone to a concert, or participated in a discussion that had you thinking the next day about something exciting and new? Of course you have. That new lyric or unexpected editorial insight got your attention, made you wonder, and sometimes had you feeling inspired.

When I first heard the Beatles song "Eight Days a Week," the title confused me (I was pretty young). After I shook my head trying to figure out how that mistake made its way into that popular song, I realized that the "error" was actually a clever way to make an interesting point: the narrator of the song spends all his time (or at least more than usual) thinking about the object of his affection. What an evocative way to express that thought!

Now we're not all geniuses like John Lennon, but we don't need to be geniuses to come up with good ideas on our own. In fact, we are idea generators throughout our lives, every day. One might say we're often responding to "prompts" that we give ourselves in trying to figure out how to face challenges, exploit opportunities, and make investigations about questions that intrigue us.

As an example, let's imagine this series of questions you might ask yourself while standing in line for a coffee on the way to class or to work:

Prompt	Response/Line of Inquiry
Does that new coffee drink being made by the barista taste good?	That woman ahead of me just ordered it. Maybe I'll ask her what it tastes like?
Why is that drink so expensive?	Is it because of the quality of the drink? The ingredients? The time it takes to make it? The neighborhood where the café is located?
How did some coffee drinks become so trendy and chic?	It seems that coffee in old movies was often the same—cheap and black. Cappuccino has probably been around a while in restaurants, but when did sidewalk cafés begin to sell it? When did teens start drinking coffee a lot?

Prompt	Response/Line of Inquiry
Coffee has been around for a while. What explains its popularity around the world?	When did coffee "begin," exactly? When did it become really popular around the world? Why has it remained so popular? Are there some cultures that really don't like coffee? What do people of those cultures drink in the morning? Does popularity vary according to gender?
I bet a lot of people would like to know the answer to the question "Who discovered coffee?"	Coffee must be cultivated in pretty large batches and roasted before a lot of people can drink it. Who was the first person to roast coffee beans in large quantities? How did people figure out that process?

If you had to stay for some time to wait in line for your coffee, it's conceivable that you could consider all these issues and questions—many of which could be the beginning or even the primary focus of an interesting essay or short research paper for high school– or college-level work.

A key caveat in this step is to make sure the idea or theme

that you eventually choose to shape a composition is not too broad; otherwise, it might require an unreasonable amount of research or argumentation. Lots of very interesting topics are far beyond the scope of a typical class assignment. For instance, answering the question "What explains the popularity of coffee around the world?" would require a lot of research to cover all the regional variations and then some degree of analysis to figure out similarities and differences between those regions. In contrast, the question "Who discovered coffee?" might be easier to tackle in a typical college paper because the question is more narrowly defined and, therefore, would probably be easier to research and master.

The "prompts" in the table above provide strong hints about some generic questions that you can use to start exploring any possible theme or issue:

- What do I know about this topic?
- What do I not know about this topic but want to learn?
- What confuses me about the topic?
- What about this topic inspires me?
- Would others also find these issues interesting?

When writers answer these questions (as we can see in the example of the coffee shop), useful insights, questions, and unknowns will arise. This is the stage of ideation that might be compared to the wide end of a funnel, when you gather as many options as you can. The one that you choose, ultimately, is an idea to fuel your interest in the topic. When you've chosen that focus, writing turns from an uphill battle into a more straightforward and interesting exploration.

Part II: Choose an Idea and Dig Deep

Your goal is to transform the writing process from being a "push" originating from a manager or an instructor to becoming a "pull" that excites your own interest. And because you are a generator of ideas ...

This approach is appropriate for more sophisticated work, too. Coffee could be the focus of many probing lines of inquiry across a college curriculum, for instance. Here are some examples of potential assignments using coffee a focus.

Science

- How does coffee interact with and stimulate the senses—the taste and smell receptors connecting the intake of coffee to the brain?
- What are the stimulating effects of caffeine? What are the costs and benefits of consuming caffeine for the human body?
- Do the stimulations from chemical caffeine and the stimulation of senses (like the sense of smell) work together to affect individuals? If not, why not? If so, how so?
- How did coffee first appear in nature? How does the creation of the coffee bean benefit the coffee plant as well as the animals that consume coffee beans?

Economics and International Trade

- How does coffee fit into the balance of trade between the Northern and Southern Hemispheres since 2010?

- A large coffee at Dunkin' Donuts costs $2.09. How did the company arrive at that price? What are the supply and demand forces that make that price acceptable to the consumer while allowing the company to make an acceptable amount of profit for its shareholders?
- The United Nations began the International Coffee Organization in 1963 to stabilize prices because of the importance of coffee production to many emerging economies. In your view, has the organization been largely successful or unsuccessful in attaining this goal in the twenty-first century? What are the arguments against stabilizing prices?

History

- The first coffeehouse in England was opened in 1652. Individual coffeehouses tended to attract clients with common occupations or interests (political affiliations, professions, artistic pursuits). Why did this self-segregation take place?
- In 1942, Maxwell House coffee was included in the rations for US soldiers. How did that decision come about? What were the effects of that decision on the United States? Your answer might focus either on the culture or on the economy of the United States.
- The mass production of coffee in Central and South America has had significant environmental impacts throughout the region. Today, a debate about coffee horticulture centers on farmers choosing between shade-grown and sun-grown coffee. What are the differences between the two? Why do the differences matter? Can you recommend some best

practices in coffee cultivation based on what you've learned about the two methods of growing coffee?

Now let's generate some options for ideas concerning one of these college-level subjects using the series of generic questions listed above. Let's focus on the topic of comparing shade-grown and sun-grown coffee by looking at the sustainability of coffee production.*

- **What do I know about this topic?**
  - I know that growing coffee requires tapping a lot of natural resources, like water and soil.
- **What do I not know about this topic but want to learn?**
  - Are there other potential kinds of coffee cultivation? Or do these two kinds of coffee growing represent the only two choices?
  - What are other important influences on coffee production: altitude, humidity, rainfall, sunlight, temperature? Are there other factors?
- **What confuses me about the topic?**
  - Which aspects of cultivating coffee are sustainable, and which parts are not? For instance, doesn't coffee always make demands on local water supplies, no matter how it's cultivated?

---

* For some more information on this topic, see Sarah Sax, "Coffee as We Know It Is in Danger. Can We Breed a Better Cup?," *Vox*, November 9, 2021, https://www.vox.com/down-to-earth/22763947/coffee-breeding-agroforestry-stenophylla-climate-leaf-rust; and Victoria Moore, "The Environmental Impact of Coffee Production: What's Your Coffee Costing the Planet?," Sustainable Business Toolkit, May 21, 2021, https://www.sustainablebusinesstoolkit.com/environmental-impact-coffee-trade/.

- **What about this topic inspires me?**
  - I never thought about how much farmers and policy makers have to consider in approaching coffee growing.
  - Learning more about this very specific kind of agriculture opens my eyes to how complex and important agricultural issues are.
- **Would others also find these issues interesting?**
  - Although I'm not a coffee fanatic, I know many who are. I'd imagine they would be interested in many details about how their favorite drink is actually created.
  - This overview of coffee cultivation could be attractive to many who are interested in sustainable food production.

You may already see how this stage of ideation relates to some aspects of the one-idea rule. In answering the last of the series of questions above, writers are already imagining the audience they're having a "conversation" with, which helps to narrow the scope of the topic (the "one idea") they will eventually explore.

So, if you were to receive a prompt for a writing assignment that said "Discuss coffee," you would probably be justified to complain that the prompt is uninspired. That might very well be true. However, a bad prompt does not mean that the broader topic lying underneath that prompt is boring, too. In fact, most topics contain some elements that can spark your interest as well as the interest of your reader. Make it *your* responsibility to find that interesting aspect to inspire yourself before you dive into an assignment. Use those generic questions above to get you started on that path.

If you can find that motivating idea, your output will almost inevitably improve. It's not a magic formula; it's a repeatable approach that begins with a writer's own curiosity, which makes written assignments more meaningful.

Part III: Confronting and Overcoming Writing Aversion

When people feel uncomfortable about or resistant to writing, that discomfort often originates from the very beginning of the assignment. If they give in to that aversion at that moment, they then step on a very slippery slope of writing problems (some of which are explored below in this section). That is why searching for *and finding* an idea that can motivate you to actually start composing and then to push through the inevitable challenges that arise while completing a composition is the most important aspect of writing.

Because ideation often precedes even starting the first sentence of a document, it can also seem to be very intangible. It's not as concrete and well defined as improving the topic sentence of a paragraph or changing the flow of an argument in an essay. Facing a blank paper or a blinking cursor on a computer screen, people responding to assignments might feel like they're being asked to create something from nothing at the snap of a finger. The worst outcome of writing aversion is that it makes people forget about their very real potential as idea generators.

But by understanding how aversion undercuts ideation, you can learn helpful habits and useful approaches that can placate negative feelings about writing so you can feel curious and confident about most writing tasks.

- **Set aside adequate time to achieve the best writing experience possible.** Writing takes time because it's a multi-faceted process and because writers often discover new ideas and insights as they are writing.

- **Write about a topic of interest to avoid many composition problems before they begin.** If you have to put effort into something you don't care about, it's likely that the final product won't be well written. Many important details in finishing a writing assignment—of clarity, logic, and grammar—will be overlooked if you're indifferent about the answer to a question or prompt.

- **Expect to make changes during the writing process.** Having an aversion to writing is closely related to the reluctance many people feel about adjusting their initial ideas or revising more developed ones after they've written a couple of pages. They might believe that the idea they started with is too "hard won" to change or abandon. Or perhaps they believe it's the only idea they can come up with and that there's no time to create another. This pessimism about reconsidering one's written work would be merited only if it were true that all writers usually finish their work on a topic without a second thought. While some pieces of writing might be works of genius, they have never, ever begun that way. In fact, the more ambitious the goal, the more changes a writer usually makes along the way.

- **While writing, practice patience.** Good writing almost always requires patience—patience *and* steady pacing. Writing well usually results from keeping a balance between allowing enough time to calmly think about alternatives and improvements to an argument *and* maintaining the momentum of thought to allow for insights and associations to emerge from concentration. Practicing patience is fundamental to making writing more fun as well as less stressful. Ideally, you should be simultaneously both a critic and cheerleader of your own work: excited with a turn of phrase at the end of an evening but waking up with a better alternative in the morning (for instance). Trusting in this patient approach allows more ideas and alternatives to unfold easily and naturally.

- **If writer's block becomes a recurring problem and makes you fear the writing process, there are many ways to shake things up and get going again.** One way to overcome lack of movement is, literally, to move. If you feel exasperated and soldered to your chair, then find a way to change your scenery. Another way to get things going with a writing assignment stuck in neutral is to find productive ways to review your in-progress work in order to see it slightly differently. A reliable method is to recast your writing in outline form, paragraph by paragraph, idea by idea. This can help you to see and reconsider the architecture supporting your paper. Reviewing and reading new material related to your topic can help you see things differently, too.

- **Writing is often like a marathon, so enlist your body's health in supporting the activity of your mind.** Of course, getting enough sleep so that your brain is alert and functioning well on any given day is absolutely necessary. But sleep as a part of the ideation and composing process over time is perhaps less appreciated. While describing the exact ideation mechanisms during sleep is elusive, everybody has experienced an "aha" moment concerning a nagging problem or question when they wake up first thing in the morning.*

Conclusion: *Terras Irradient*

It may sound like a mantra by now, but this chapter's indispensable underlying theme concerns the advantages of concentrating on doing one thing at a time.† From biking, to reading, to working, to listening, we generally observe and perform things better if we give those things our full attention. In writing, that means striving to discuss or prove *one* major theme, not many, and aligning supporting arguments and evidence behind that theme.

---

* One scientist has posited an interesting evolutionary explanation for the unconscious brain's version of ideation, which is dreaming: it helps us to be prepared for future scenarios that may arise, scenarios patched together with various scraps of recent experience. "The fact that no more than 20% of dream material is in any way related to what the dreamer recollects of events in his or her life history indicates that dreaming could represent a set of foreordained scripts or scenarios for the organization of our waking experience. According to this hypothesis, our brains are as much creative artists as they are copy editors. What we may need to navigate our waking world is an infinite set of charts from which we may draw the one best suited to an equally infinite set of real-life possibilities. To this end, it makes sense to tie even remotely connected scraps of experience together to give our library of plots enough verisimilitude to be useful." See J. Allan Hobson, "REM sleep and dreaming: Towards a theory of protoconsciousness," *Nature Reviews Neuroscience* 10 (November 2009): 803-13.

† As one writer has put it, "Doing several things at once is a trick we play on ourselves, thinking we're getting more done. In reality, our productivity goes down by as much as 40%. We don't actually multitask. We switch-task, rapidly shifting from one thing to another, interrupting ourselves unproductively, and losing time in the process." See Peter Bregman, "How (and Why) to Stop Multitasking," *Harvard Business Review*, May 20, 2010, https://hbr.org/2010/05/how-and-why-to-stop-multitaski.

The exciting thing about concentration on a certain topic is that writers will often manage to be surprised by discoveries and connections they make as they write over a period of time with concentration. It's truly amazing. Writers can begin a line of inquiry in a paper having a somewhat strong idea about the evidence they can use and about the arguments drawn from them. Then, sometimes at a very unexpected moment, an insight or a connection *one has never made before* suddenly appears in the mind. Maybe it's only a half-formed insight, and perhaps the idea will eventually be proven wrong. But at the time, it feels almost like a spontaneous act of creation—a "little bang"—that seems as bright as a bolt of lightning, with an energy that might be able to open up a whole new world. And sometimes, it does.

Review and Apply: Ideation

- Apply your everyday problem-solving skills (i.e., responding to challenges, opportunities, and intriguing questions) to developing ideas for a writing assignment.
- Although the ultimate goal in ideation is to discuss *one* idea or theme that is relatively narrow and well defined, start out by exploring many possible themes that excite your curiosity.
- From these themes, choose one that gives you motivation to write more about your chosen topic.
- Once a theme is defined, start to ask questions about it as a way to search for narrower paths of exploration that do not demand more time and/or expertise than you possess at the time of writing.

- If you feel an aversion to writing that prevents you from taking the time to find a motivating idea, remember that this aversion is often derived from the reluctance many people feel about adjusting their initial ideas after they've spent some time working on them. But making changes to a piece of writing—from small tweaks to starting over with a revised theme—is a natural part of discovery resulting from concentration. As long as you remember that your final product should be supporting only one main theme or idea, making adjustments along the way should not be particularly problematic.

Chapter 5

Composing

∙∙∙

Part I: Choose a Writing Framework, or Create One

Almost every piece of writing can be described as a kind of story, shaped by a beginning, a middle, and an end. This three-part structure is often described as a "narrative arc." The image of the arc was probably adopted because its "summit" symbolizes the hardest part of the story for the writer (as well as the reader) to "reach." While approaching that summit, the explanation of an idea or events can become a little "steeper" or more difficult—either more complicated in a work of nonfiction or more tense or uncertain in a work of fiction. In contrast, the opening and the ending of a narrative should be relatively easier (or less "steep") for a writer to manage, with the opening introducing a topic and the ending providing a conclusion.

After the opening of an expository or argumentative piece of writing has done its work by describing the goal that the writer intends to reach by the end, the challenging longer part—the middle section—begins. The middle of a story requires some effort, consistent focus, and healthy self-criticism to be accomplished successfully.

For very young students in elementary and middle school, learning how to write a story with a narrative arc can be very challenging. Teaching good writing habits to kids who may find it difficult or boring to focus on a single topic for an extended time is also quite a challenge for teachers. Responding to that difficulty, many teachers (at least in the United States) have used a framework that offers a ready-made structure for students, which is known as the five-paragraph essay. This framework does offer a steady and reliable way for students to cultivate a topic while helping to avoid detours or rambling, but it also has some strong liabilities. I learned this lesson the hard way as a sophomore in college.

Moving Beyond the Five-Paragraph Essay

During the spring of my sophomore year at college, I enrolled in a survey of American literature cotaught by two rock stars of the English department, Professors Dale Peterson and Kim Townsend. About six weeks later, I was eager to learn about my professor's reaction to my first long paper (ten to twelve pages) in the class. I don't remember the topic of that assignment anymore, but I vividly remember the grade. It was a C-. The main critique I received from my professor was that he couldn't really distinguish one important, central argument that I was supporting (the "one idea" that is the foundation of any good paper).

Looking back a few months later (after I got over the shock of that bad grade), I think I understood what went wrong: I had become too dependent on using the structure of the five-paragraph essay. It had worked for so long during high school, and it hadn't occurred to me that I might need any other approach.

If you're reading this and feel like this story is familiar to you, you're not alone. The five-paragraph essay has demonstrated great power in shaping the habits of young writers. But many writers have become victims of its success and have not explored other kinds of frameworks that might help to expand their options and improve their arguments.

The framework I was outgrowing that year at college was made up of three very dependable parts:

A. An opening paragraph that declared what the essay would demonstrate in a thesis statement briefly outlining three supporting arguments (or pieces of evidence)

B. Three paragraphs in the body of the paper, each taking up the supporting arguments in the order they had appeared in the first paragraph

C. A concluding paragraph

During high school, I began writing papers longer than five paragraphs. My strategy to write long papers was to start with that old, familiar approach and then stretch it as far as it could go. I'd open, of course, with that classic first paragraph. Then, instead of offering one paragraph per supporting argument, I might create three paragraphs per argument, or even more. This approach wasn't necessarily comfortable, but I didn't think of alternatives to structuring an expository or argumentative essay. When I wrote that C-paper, the meandering passages and vague arguments were derived from my attempt to write about more complicated issues than those I had mastered in high school. I was trying to explore deeper questions or insights. These needed better packaging—a more useful arrangement—than I had given my ideas before.

This experience taught me that original thoughts generally don't fit well into a highly structured template, especially if it becomes formulaic. In other words, becoming dependent on a framework means that writers will conform their thinking to the demands of that framework. Instead, writers need to choose (or, in some cases, create) a framework that best supports their thinking. Of course, very young writers can and do benefit from becoming familiar with the five-paragraph essay. Its rock-solid construction offers a great way for people to get in the habit of creating a "narrative arc" in all their writing. Its main weakness is that is does not allow for the discovery of new ideas during the writing process. (Discovery will be discussed more in the second half of this chapter). In short, the structure of the five-paragraph essay, though stout, is a small one; it can't contain big ideas.

While the inflexibility of the five-paragraph essay is generally confining for writers as they mature, that is not the case for all rigid frameworks. For instance, the structure of most scientific papers is extremely formulaic, but for good reason. Because the substance and explanations of scientific research can be extremely complex, scientists have come up with an almost universal framework for discussing scientific research with peers. The influential scientific journal *Nature* describes the framework this way: "Papers that report experimental work are often structured chronologically in five sections: first, *Introduction*; then *Materials and Methods*, *Results*, and *Discussion* (together, these three sections make up the paper's body); and finally, *Conclusion*."* The positive contribution made by this framework is to funnel both research and the discussion of that

---

* "Scientific Papers," Scitable by Nature Education, accessed January 6, 2023, https://www
.nature.com/scitable/topicpage/scientific-papers-13815490/#:~:text=Papers%20that%20
report%20experimental%20work,body)%3B%20and%20finally%2C%20Conclusion.

research into narrow pathways that help writers avoid pursuing the many potential paths of complication or interest. At the same time, the framework assists readers in finding (or returning to) certain parts of the paper that are of particular interest. This can minimize idiosyncratic variation in writing styles that could detract from the subject of primary interest: discoveries uncovered by rigorous research and experimentation.

Allowing Ideas to Develop

In contrast to the rigidity of the five-paragraph essay, I've constructed a very different framework that is designed precisely for those difficult problems that the five-paragraph essay is poorly equipped to handle. Instead of the limited menu of options offered by the five-paragraph essay, approaching an essay as a series of questions and answers (or "Q&A") about a theme or a thesis can open up some interesting narrative possibilities while still helping writers to keep a focus on their "one idea."

Here's my "Q&A" outline:

A. Announce the main idea/theme.
B. Explore related and supporting issues.
   i. Bring up problems and paradoxes related to the main idea.
   ii. Offer responses and resolutions.

Like the five-paragraph essay, the Q&A outline has three parts—a beginning, middle, and end. Unlike the five-paragraph essay, however, the opening paragraph does not necessarily provide a brief outline of the rest of the paper. Its job is to declare a goal or end point that the writer will guide the reader toward. Also distinct is the indeterminate amount of supporting arguments that will be brought up in the body of the piece.

Composing with the intent of exploring the questions and answers of issues related to the main idea gives you freedom to write as much or as little as you desire concerning any of the questions encountered in the essay. And because you are exploring questions or puzzles (and not just providing a list of three supporting arguments), you are more likely to grab the attention of the reader.

Consider two contrasting frameworks used for a piece with the theme of *finding a pet that best suits apartment living in an urban center*. We'll start with the five-paragraph essay framework.

A composition shaped by this title could be prescriptive and offer an outline of a method to find the best pet for an apartment: "These three tips can help you make a decision." Because this follows the style of the five-paragraph essay framework, the resulting essay will likely be very clear, but it will probably offer fewer opportunities for exploration.

In contrast, the piece could begin more tentatively, with the author being clearer about the question than the possible answers. This kind of writing might resemble the more relaxed style you would encounter in a blog post on a site like Apartment Therapy or Rent.com:*

I'd really like a big dog, but it isn't realistic. But what kind of pet should I look for instead? I've asked friends and family about this issue. I've read a few articles and skimmed through several

---

* Apartment Therapy can be found at https://www.apartmenttherapy.com/. For a listicle on a similar theme, see Claire Tak, "The Best Cities for Pets," Rent.com (blog), December 29, 2020, https://www.rent.com/blog/best-cities-for-pets/.

YouTube videos. There are a lot of contradictory views out there. It's frustrating.

The opening is clear: it focuses on a person who is indecisive or torn about a choice he has to make. At this point, without the planning of the five-paragraph essay, the blog post could take on many directions, so long as it remains focused on either exploring or answering the main issue (or its "one idea") brought up in the opening: the difficulty this writer has in making a decision about acquiring a pet suitable for an apartment.

An outline for the beginning of a more exploratory piece answering the question could look like this:

A. "How to Pick the Right Pet for Your Living Situation? One Person's Experience..."
   i. Writer did research about pets and also asked friends and family.
   ii. In sum, information was inconclusive.
B. The writer wants a pet because of the close relationships he had with two dogs while growing up.
   i. The big dog, a collie, loved running with him while he rode his bike.
   ii. The little dog, a bichon frise, would cuddle with him at night.
C. The writer's childhood experiences don't offer him good choices in his city apartment.
   i. Big dogs need lots of exercise, so he'd have to spend a lot of time on walks.
   ii. Little dogs can tend to be nervous or bark a lot, which could bother the neighbors while the dog is home alone.

D. The writer thinks of getting a cat instead of a dog.
   i. He has not had a lot of experience with cats.
   ii. They're easier to take care of in an apartment.
   iii. His friend at work has a cat, so he will ask if he can visit her apartment and see what an owner has to do to take care of indoor cats.

If the writer can maintain a focus on the main issue, readers will generally indulge the writer with his exploration of secondary issues (like the writer's childhood experiences with pets), so long as the primary theme does not recede too far into the background.

Of course, writers often take big detours in their work or lose track entirely of their primary theme. If you notice this happening in a piece of writing you're working on, there are generally two courses of action: (1) delete that detour; (2) reconsider the primary focus of the essay. Either decision will improve your essay, but you need to decide one way or another so that your essay ends up clearly focusing on *one* main idea.

In the case of this blog post, imagine that the writer's visit to his friend's apartment was entertaining but still inconclusive. He writes that he then walked home and started fantasizing about riding in a luxury BMW. Riding in a luxury car is only tangentially connected to the theme of choosing a pet, and because this draft of his post began by discussing pets, the focus has now become blurry.

To make the focus of the writing sharp again, the writer can delete the section about the car and return to the discussion of pets. But there is another alternative. If the writer was somehow very drawn to the discussion of the BMW, that may be a signal that there's a new topic that might interest the writer more. Maybe, instead of focusing on choosing a pet, there is another, new theme that is emerging from this draft. The theme could include a wider discussion of leisure activities. Or it could be an essay about the problems faced by a person who daydreams a lot and changes his mind frequently. All of these options are viable so long as they are shaped by one idea. In contrast, a piece of writing about choosing a pet *and* fantasizing about luxury cars actually contains two main ideas; therefore, it's guaranteed not to be successful, unless it's revised.

The most important lesson to be drawn from this story about choosing themes for a piece of writing is this: *writers can explore many possible goals for their work, but they can only end up at one destination.*

Part II: The Utility of Frameworks: Maintaining Focus on One Idea and Facilitating Transitions

One advantage of consciously choosing a framework to create the overall shape of a document is that it can act as a constant reminder to the writer of that document's main theme. The structure of any framework *always* begins with that central idea.

As implied in the earlier discussions of the five-paragraph essay and Q&A framework, each framework contains an implicit or explicit logical approach to creating a meaningful sequence of topics that support an argument—a sequence that also offers the reader a way to understand the meaning of the material as a whole. Thanks to the logical sequence of material, many transitions can already be "baked into" a document without the writer making them explicit.

Here are five frameworks you can use, along with some examples of how they may be appropriate for different kinds of documents.

The Five-Paragraph Essay Framework

This is the most basic framework and simply highlights three points that will be discussed to support the main theme. The framework doesn't add a lot to the argument, but usually the reader gets exactly what the writer promises at the outset.

Because this framework simply presents material without promising any particular logic to uphold an argument, it would be appropriate in shaping documents from a source whose authority is unquestioned or will probably not be questioned. A private club's description of a dress code or its rules of conduct might be usefully shaped by the five-paragraph framework:

> Welcome to the Elk's Horn Country Club, and congratulations on becoming a new member. We anticipate that you'll enjoy your time here, and we look forward to getting to know you better.
>
> To make sure that you and your fellow club members feel comfortable and relaxed whenever you come to visit, we encourage everyone to follow some simple rules of thumb concerning three issues that have an impact on the club atmosphere: attire, closing hours, and guest policies.

In these kinds of instances, the reader is not looking for evidence of the writer's intelligence or research because the writer requires no supporting evidence to make their assertions. Instead of a logical sequence, the reader is looking for a clear description of rules so that they can maintain membership in a club. Readers can accept or reject these assertions, of course, but the writer is not obliged to engage the readers in a discussion to convince them to accept the assertions. Likewise, a description of personal preferences or experiences (e.g., "Why I Love Spicy Foods" or "Some Amazing Insights from My High School English Teacher") doesn't necessarily need a logical structure to be shared with others.*

The Q&A Framework

As discussed earlier in this chapter, the Q&A framework is an exploratory approach to discussing a topic. What keeps the essay coherent is the relationship from one question to the next while exploring a topic.

The Q&A framework does not promise any answers in particular, but strings together a series of tentative insights and intriguing problems around an issue. Because the ultimate outcome of reading a document shaped by this framework can feel tentative or incomplete, the writer needs to be all the more attentive to keeping the discussion focused on its main theme. This is often appropriate for issues that are new to the writer or for issues that are evolving and whose contours are unclear for the moment. This format could be adopted, for instance, by an editorial writer or journalist covering a recent issue or problem. For instance, the headline "Earthquake in Manila: What We Know as of Today" concerns information that is incomplete or "in progress" but that readers nevertheless feel is important to know now. An article written a day after the earthquake might gather information in categories that collectively give a broad overview of the situation without necessarily developing an

---

* Please note that while a logical structure is not always necessary in a document, it can often act as an intellectual hook to keep the reader's interest until the end of a discussion because it promises that all the material shaped by that structure will be pertinent to understanding the main idea.

argument. These categories could include: strength and location of the earthquake, cities affected, approximate death toll, rescue operations, and the government's priorities during the next three days.

The Chronological Framework

As discussed above, this format simply explains a topic according to a sequence of events or steps over time. Chronologies can be used quickly within other kinds of essay frameworks when a series of events needs to be explained. But a chronology can also provide the primary framework for an entire document.

Chronological frameworks are particularly well suited for subjects that require step-by-step instructions for future actions or explanations for past actions. Documents that might employ this framework to good effect include manuals for creating something that is somewhat complicated (like building a telescope or making a complicated main course for a meal).

A chronology framework can also be leveraged to reconstruct a series of events that usually lead to a culmination point. This might be done, for instance, in a legal brief when a lawyer tries to get a jury or judge to understand the circumstances that led up to a problem now faced by a client. A chronology could also help order and describe various issues that led up to an accident. Scientists often employ a chronology to explain natural phenomena, like a volcanic eruption or the progress of a deadly disease. Historians often use chronologies to explain the buildup to historical events (although histories that rely too much on chronologies can seem monotonous without attempting some kind of explanation or interpretation to search for causes or meaning that emerge from the chronology).

Like the five-paragraph essay, the chronological framework is very clear, but it does not have much explanatory power or potential embedded in it. One thing happening after another is a pretty simplified way of understanding the world around us. Nevertheless, if a chronology is used in appropriate contexts, it can provide a very reliable and powerful way to understand some phenomena—especially if the sequence of events leading up to an important moment or action is poorly understood or in dispute (opposing sides in a courtroom often argue vehemently about the correct ordering of events concerning an issue).

The Prioritization Framework

This format creates an argument that follows some sort of prioritization, a sequence that has its own logic: bigger to smaller, adjacent to distant, etc. In contrast to the five-paragraph and chronological frameworks, creating a sequence according to priorities is neither arbitrary (as with the five-paragraph essay) nor obvious (like a chronology). The priorities are usually created or chosen by the author and should serve some explanatory purpose that enhances or clarifies the information contained in a document. Taking up an old phrase that seems apt, prioritization makes the whole greater than the sum of the parts (and not just orderly).

Documents and instructions for emergency situations almost always use a prioritization structure beginning with a first step that is crucial in emergency response. If the main idea in emergency instructions is to save lives, then that first step taken during an emergency may make the difference between life and death. For CPR (cardiopulmonary resuscitation), checking that the victim's airway is open must come before attempting chest compressions. Audiences in crowded auditoriums are often told to locate the nearest exit before a show begins to prevent them from searching for one during the confusion of an actual emergency. And some of the most famous first steps in an emergency involve adults and children flying together in an airplane. When passengers need to put on oxygen masks, instructions for putting them on go against the most fundamental parental instinct, which is protecting one's child above all other considerations: "Make sure to secure your mask first before helping with your child's mask." Airlines certainly must have learned from hard experience that parental instinct isn't always adapted to airplane travel. Many children must have ended up endangered because a parent became incapacitated while trying to get a struggling child to wear an oxygen mask.

A prioritization that begins with a foundational element at the beginning of a document is the Declaration of Independence, written by Thomas Jefferson in 1776. After an introductory paragraph, Jefferson proclaims, "We hold these truths to be self-evident, that all men are created equal . . ." From this statement, all the ensuing smaller declarations are derived (e.g., "That to secure these rights, Governments are instituted among Men . . .") and would probably not make sense without that foundational statement. Written during the Enlightenment era, Jefferson's prioritization could also be described as "deductive reasoning," which begins with a central idea or premise and explores ideas derived from it. Not surprisingly, deductive reasoning is used in lots of philosophy, which often tries to demonstrate truth through logical exploration of the implications of a premise.

The cousin of deductive reasoning is inductive reasoning, a prioritization framework that ends with the most important idea instead of beginning with it. Leaving the most important idea until the end can make for very interesting reading (as the reader wonders and guesses where a line of argument is leading to), but it is the most sophisticated kind of prioritization. Doing this requires the writer to guide the reader with care by keeping the main idea (and many of its implications) very clearly in mind throughout the piece. The French philosopher René Descartes uses inductive reasoning to dramatic effect as he recounts his search for philosophical certainty. At the end of much effort and anxiety in *Discourse on the Method*, he finally finds his (now famous) first principle, "I think; therefore, I am."

The Logical/Argumentative Framework

Because argumentative documents are often dedicated to proving a point (and not just describing or exploring an issue), they must create an argument that is logically sound. And if somebody is proving a point, it's often in opposition to popular beliefs or practices. In other words, a person writing an argumentative piece is usually trying to prove that somebody else is wrong, so their arguments will probably undergo close scrutiny for errors from unfriendly or skeptical readers. So, the logical steps of argumentation (e.g., this problem leads to this question, which then leads to this possible solution) also function, in effect, as transitions.

Editorials or opinion pieces often take the form of argumentative essays and usually do so by taking issue with very specific pieces of public policy or opinion. In fact, newspapers sometimes critique each other; in October 2022, the editorial board of the *Chicago Tribune* called out the *New York Times* for criticizing the politicians asking for aid from the federal government in the wake of Hurricane Ian who had *also* argued against climate change being a significant problem. Notice in the following excerpt how the *Tribune* editorial is careful to quote directly from the source it is critiquing, allowing the *Times* to speak for itself concerning its "one idea" about the hypocrisy of certain politicians in Florida asking for aid:

> Americans expect all hands on deck in a crisis, and they expect help to go to those who need it in the moment, regardless of their race or the contents of their bank accounts. It behooves high ranking officials to shut up about everything else.
>
> You might argue the same about the media. "Gov. Ron DeSantis and other Florida Republicans rejected major climate laws," said the *New York Times* in an especially churlish and clueless gotcha-tweet from dry Manhattan. "Now they're seeking storm aid."

Then the *Tribune* quickly makes a riposte to the *Times* assertion, which also acts as a transition to the next logical point (i.e., the solution to the problem of attacking people who seek aid after an emergency):

> Well, duh. Of course they are [seeking storm aid]. As they should. That is their duty to their citizens who just lost most everything, as it is our duty as Americans to come to their aid.*

Whatever approach a writer takes to organizing the flow or sequence of an essay, it's always best to have *some* sort of sequence or

---

* Editorial Board of the *Chicago Tribune*, "Hold the Condescending Lectures. Give Hurricane Aid to Everyone in Need," *Chicago Tribune*, October 5, 2022, https://www.chicagotribune.com/opinion/editorials/ct-editorial-hurricane-aid-ian-florida-20221005-w4s2pocbbjaijm6nqaqicc732q-story.html.

framework in mind. Different sequences or orderings of arguments and evidence have different implications for the development of pieces of writing. No one framework is really better than the other, per se. They're only better suited for the writer's intent. So, a writer starting off with a chronological framework may eventually find it to be unsatisfactory and will then turn to a framework based on prioritization. The key thing is to find a framework that best enhances the discussion and/or proof of the main idea.

Part III: Writing Always Entails Discovery

The discussion of the in-progress blog post about choosing a pet offers an instance of discovery and improvement made by a writer during the process of composing. However, reassessing an idea and recalibrating a paragraph (or more) can be perceived by many as a task that costs precious time and energy. Pauses can seem to be roadblocks when writers are too committed to the first articulation of their theme or main idea. Holding on to that goal too firmly can make these reconsiderations seem like mini crises on the road to the planned completion of a written assignment.

However, if these pauses are considered differently, they may promote better outcomes. Instead of obstacles, they can be perceived as very normal and natural crossroads of new potential ideas that writers always encounter on the way toward a completed assignment. These crossroads appear because writing forces us to articulate convictions, beliefs, and hunches that we haven't been previously forced to support with complete statements.

As an illustration of how ideas can unfold to improve initial insights or conclusions, consider the misconceptions many believed during the early days of man-powered flight. Some aviation pioneers made a plausible guess that people could imitate bird flight by flapping their arms and launching themselves airborne (with the help of a larger version of bird wings). This first hunch, of course, proved itself to be unworkable and soon gave way to the fixed-wing aircraft first perfected by the Wright brothers.

The parallel connecting the early days of flight to writing is that writers may likewise convince themselves that their first idea is sound—or the best idea they can come up with. But if they ignore promising alternatives that arise in response to difficulties presented to their argument along the way, they may also set themselves up for a disappointment or even a flop. One of the great advantages of making sure your sentences are grammatically sound is that complete sentences act as helpful tests to your thinking, *one idea at a time!*

These tests can have both small-scale and large-scale impact. Recalling the blog post earlier on choosing a pet, the writer may have begun the exploration of this topic without having anticipated also looking into the positive and negative aspects of owning a cat. Including cats in this paper topic expands focus to dogs *and* cats and also opens the door to considering other kinds of pets. This is a small-scale change because the expansion of the topic still keeps the paper focused on looking at animals as pets. A possibility for larger-scale change of the main idea occurred when the writer made a possible move from a focus on pets to the theme of leisure activities.

If a writer eventually decides to change the focus of their essay significantly, they may have to start over, usually with a new first paragraph. Luckily, this is not a problem. What the writer has discovered is an idea that is more interesting and more engaging.

As was mentioned in the previous chapter, being engaged with the topic of one's writing usually translates into better work that's easier to produce. With renewed energy derived from a more interesting topic, it's pretty easy for writers to begin with a modified version of an earlier argument. They simply have a new principal topic or theme to use as their "one idea" that they will use to shape and direct their writing going forward. Writing with the gentle discipline of the one-idea rule can give writers the confidence to change direction without fearing that they will suffer a major "penalty" for making these changes that are a perfectly natural outcome of discoveries made while composing.

Leveraging Counterarguments

Writers are sometimes reluctant to face the possible contradictions to their arguments. It can seem a lot easier to forge ahead with a certain point of view and ignore an argument's weaknesses or shortcomings and concentrate on cultivating its strengths.

While it can be demanding to face negative critiques in the short term, accounting for the weaknesses in your own writing has two great payoffs in the long run. Firstly, your argument becomes much more convincing when it confronts its possible shortcomings—shortcomings that will have occurred to many of your readers. Secondly, dealing with counterarguments is a form of ideation! While this happens mainly during the composition process (because that is when many counterarguments may surface in the mind of the writer), confronting criticism immediately gives a writer new ideas to explore. Moreover, these counterarguments are, almost by definition, tightly connected to the main argument because they are made in opposition to that argument.

Strong counterarguments have one more underappreciated virtue: they can often inspire great insights and eloquence in the writer who has to overcome them. Remember that every argument (like any choice in life), no matter how strong, has some weakness, some trade-off embedded in it. Nothing is perfect. And, often, the bolder and more visionary an argument, the more exposed it becomes to criticism because of its novelty or its ambitiousness. If a writer does not want to abandon a grand idea, then confronting criticism usually becomes the writer's task. If that task is formidable, rising to meet it usually demands reflection and creativity. And in the pressure of that confrontation, a writer's eloquence may emerge as the last defense against a formidable challenge. Those moments aren't commonplace, but they are highly satisfying.

In some cases, a counterargument may be so convincing that a writer decides to abandon the original discussion altogether. There's certainly nothing wrong or shameful about that. Reason, logic, and persuasion should reign supreme in the best of circumstances. Our ideas are indeed precious, but our willingness to truly consider alternative points of view (with potentially better evidence or arguments) is even more important. Without openness to hearing about the weaknesses in our viewpoints, our minds harden and our ideas become dogma.

Conclusion: Before Packing Up Your Work, Write Down Your Next Thought

Frameworks can offer some valuable aids to writers and their readers because they allow both parties to envision the general flow of an argument within a document. Frameworks often imply not only how a document might be organized but also the way in which issues will be addressed or how questions will be answered. (Good examples of this are the prioritization frameworks used for deductive and inductive reasoning.) This element of predictability gives both writers and readers some stable intellectual ground from which to explore challenging complicated topics. The organizing potential of frameworks is extremely helpful, sometimes giving writers a "head start" on analyzing a topic by offering a way of thinking about material and presenting it to readers.

Despite this advantage offered by frameworks, writers tackling new and/or difficult material—especially under a deadline or time limit—may nevertheless run into conceptual dead ends. If you're feeling somewhat frustrated after a long round of writing or thinking, there is one way you can make the most out of your effort.

After completing a section of a paper or exploring a complicated idea, writers often feel tired and are eager to put their work away. But at that moment, writers are *also* usually "in the zone"—which is a colloquial way to describe the state of concentration resulting from focused thinking about a topic over a relatively long period of time. Being "in the zone" is a precious and unique state of mind that requires a lot of energy to create and also to recover.

It's understandable that writers are tired at this moment because they've been working hard, but they should do just a little more before moving on with their day. Writers should try to think of the next idea in their piece and describe it briefly for themselves. It could be a few bullet points, some phrases, or just a sentence. But that idea has now been at least partially captured to help the writer make an energetic start to the next writing session.

Review and Apply: Composing

- Every written document tells a story of some kind, with a beginning, middle, and end. The image often employed to represent this progression is an arc, or a "narrative arc."
- The most widely used narrative arc employed in the United States is the five-paragraph essay. This might also be understood as a writing "framework"—a ready-made "arc" that tells a story in a particular way that is also orderly and logical to the reader. There are several frameworks writers can choose from.
- You don't have to write according to a framework, but frameworks can help you choose and order the material to best support your main theme.
- As in the ideation process, composing with concentration can yield discoveries that may prompt a reevaluation of your initial theme or idea.
- Embrace those discoveries as the fruit of deep thinking, and don't worry about starting over. If you do start over, it's usually in order to accommodate better insights and ideas.
- Face counterarguments directly because doing so will strengthen your reasoning while also yielding interesting content.

Chapter 6

Refinement

....

Part I: Refinement, Step by Step

In the introduction to this book, we saw how the one-idea rule described the manner in which various components of a document (e.g., title, paragraph, sentence) should be related to one another and how they work together to support the main title or main theme. In this chapter, we will cover how best to refine a paper by keeping all those components in mind when a document is approaching completion.

There are many things that could be improved at this stage of writing, but the one-idea rule prioritizes *stating ideas clearly in a way that best supports the main theme or title of a piece*. The most important step in refinement, therefore, is to check on the alignment of ideas between the sentences, paragraphs, and the title of a document. If there's a way to make that construction stronger, then tending to those areas will yield the most fruitful results. A primary example of this is reordering paragraphs to improve the promised flow or arrangement of ideas that was implied by a certain framework. In a chronological framework, for instance, a writer might rearrange the order of paragraphs if a mistake in the order of events was made in the first draft.

The second most important step of refinement focuses on smaller segments of a document (rather than checking on its overall cohesiveness). Problems arising from these smaller segments might be described as potholes or wrong turns on the road to a writer's destination—the kinds of problems that can take readers off track and may cause them to lose sight of the main point. Some of the most typical obstacles to keeping the reader's attention on the final destination include: poor transitions between sentences, grammatical mistakes within a sentence, confusing passages of several sentences, and repetition of previously stated ideas.

The third step (which should nearly always be left until the end of the writing process) is often described as "wordsmithing." It refers to improving individual sentences with slight adjustments in an attempt to find better (or sometimes "perfect") words or phrases to express an idea.

Part II: Refinements Executed Within Five Writing Frameworks

Below are some short exercises that will help you consider and practice the first two steps of refinement. (Wordsmithing, since it should almost always be left until the end, will be discussed afterward). Some of these exercises are based on the examples used in the discussion of writing frameworks in chapter five. In each exercise, one document will be described in a partial outline. Within that outline, the reader will find one or more problems highlighted that could be improved by some sort of refinement. Readers should attempt on their own to name and solve any problems that may require refinement. Possible solutions will be offered.

The Five Paragraph–Essay Framework

Title	Topics of the first three paragraphs	Sentences within a selected paragraph
"Some Amazing Insights from My High School English Teacher"	1. Students usually rise to the expectations teachers set for them. 2. Teachers must demonstrate respect for students if they hope to be respected by them. 3. My English teacher did display a bad temper at times.	Setting high expectations is important for students. Inevitably, some students are more open to influence than others. There are certainly some limits to a teacher's capacity to make their students better.

- **Refinement 1:** Paragraphs
  - **Problem:** The third paragraph about the teacher's temper is not aligned with the title because it doesn't deal with the stated main idea promising to focus on insights offered by the teacher.
  - **Solution:** Replace with a new topic that is aligned:

"In his lectures and in his comments on our papers, he taught us that little details often mattered a lot."

- **Refinement 2:** Sentences in Paragraph 1
  - **Problem:** While the first sentence is aligned with the intended message of the first paragraph, the subsequent sentences introduce another idea, which concerns the obstacles to influencing students positively.
  - **Solution:** Develop ideas in alignment with the first sentence, then separate the remaining sentences. Sentences that are not aligned should be deleted. A revised paragraph could read as follows: "Setting high expectations is important for students. In doing so, teachers send a strong implicit message to students that they believe in their capacities to learn and achieve. A lack of this belief, a lack of confidence, is probably the most critical obstacle in the way of students achieving success."

The Q&A Framework

Title	Topics of the first three paragraphs	Sentences within a selected paragraph
"Earthquake in Manila: What We Know as of Today"	1. Yesterday, a 7.1 magnitude earthquake hit the coast of Manila.	
	2. The first goal for rescuers is to assess the damage to the city.	Information has been difficult to gather, and temperatures are
	3. With communications cut off, initial assessments can only be based on educated guesses.	rising in the tropical heat. Not even landlines connected to underground cables seemed to be working.

- **Refinement:** Sentences in Paragraph 3
  - **Problem:** The first sentence is a compound sentence that is grammatically correct; however, the second idea in that compound sentence is not related to the main topic of "communications" in the paragraph where they appear.

- **Solution:** Simply delete the clause dealing with temperatures, which leaves the passage as a single sentence: "Information has been difficult to gather." (The initial mistake may have been a result of the author desiring to add information to underline the drama of the situation in Manila. This could be the topic of another paragraph, but it is not germane to Paragraph 3, which focuses on communications.)

The Chronological Framework

Title	Topics of the first three paragraphs	Sentences within a selected paragraph
"Eradicating Smallpox: Lessons Learned from India in the 1970s"	1. India had dealt with smallpox repeatedly over the centuries. ➡ 2. In 1962, the government of India aimed to attain a vaccination rate of 100 percent of the population. 3. By 1973, India moved away from a 100 percent vaccination goal to a "surveillance and containment" strategy.	In the 1970s, India was one of the few remaining places where smallpox remained a threat for many. Even though the disease had been eradicated from large parts of the world. Inside and outside of the country, many believed that India's dense urban population centers made eradication impossible. Indeed, many conditions that enabled the spread of smallpox in India had not changed much for centuries.

- **Refinement:** Sentences in Paragraph 1
    - **Problem:** Generally, the ideas of the argument in the paragraphs and the sentences are aligned and follow a chronological order. Unfortunately, there is a sentence fragment in the first paragraph in the form of a subordinate clause that is not attached to an independent clause: "Even though the disease had been eradicated from large parts of the world." This fragment could certainly cause the reader to be confused. Not only is it an incomplete thought, but it also could be connected to the idea either in the sentence preceding it or following it. This confusion will slow down reading and make the piece less convincing.
    - **Solution:** The fragment could be deleted, leaving an intelligible paragraph. Or the fragment could be attached to one of the two ideas surrounding it. For example, "Even though the disease had been eradicated from large parts of the world, many observers inside and outside of the country believed that India's dense urban population centers made eradication impossible."

The Prioritization Framework

Title	Topics of the first three paragraphs	Sentences within a selected paragraph
"The Declaration of Independence"	1. America should explain its reasons for its radical political rupture with Great Britain to the world. 2. Because all men are created equally, they → have the right to rebel when they suffer repeated instances of abuse and injustice. 3. Here is a long list of injuries and unjust actions perpetrated by the King against the colonies.	We hold these truths to be self-evident, that all men are created equal, that they are endowed by their Creator with certain unalienable Rights, that among these are Life, Liberty and the pursuit of Happiness. — That to secure these rights, Governments are instituted among Men, deriving their just powers from the consent of the governed, —That whenever any Form of Government becomes destructive of these ends, it is the Right of the People to alter or to abolish it . . .

- **Refinement:** None. If you expected and then found any major problems with Jefferson's construction of his argument, you were led astray by the assignment . . . on purpose. Sometimes there are no major problems with a piece of writing, and we should be careful not to find mistakes simply because we might expect them to be there. Jefferson remains true to his deductive reasoning throughout the document, or at least as the document is represented in the outline above.

- **Commentary:** One critique of Jefferson's Declaration could be directed at the third part of the document, which features a long list of accusations against King George III. This is the least remembered part of the document, probably because its repetitiveness contrasts so greatly with the grace, originality, and bravado of the opening two paragraphs.

The Logical/Argumentative Framework

Title	Topics of the first three paragraphs	Sentences within a selected paragraph
Chicago Tribune Editorial: "Hold the Condescending Lectures. Give Hurricane Aid to Everyone in Need."	1. Many Chicagoans have made ⟶ Southwest Florida their home. 2. Chicago-style food and people are visible all over the area. 3. Many native Chicagoans living around Fort Myers have made great family memories in Southwest Florida.	Southwest Florida is filled with Chicagoans. In Naples, Chicago philanthropists such as the late Raymond Lutgert transformed those communities, supporting their museums and galleries. The founding CEO of the Naples Philharmonic Center for the Arts was a former Chicago advertising executive. Plenty of real estate developers from this city turned their attention to sunnier climes, later in life.

- **Refinement:** Title
  - **Problem:** The two independent sentences that make up the title of the editorial are not tightly related to one another and could suggest that the piece is about two ideas instead of one.
  - **Solution:** Create a one-sentence title. This could be done by deleting the first sentence and leaving the second one, which is the real theme of the editorial. An alternative would be to bring together those two sentences into one statement as best as one can: "Don't Berate People Who Need Help After Hurricane Ian."
- **Refinement:** Paragraphs
  - **Problem:** The three paragraphs deal with ideas that are very similar and can feel repetitious.
  - **Solution:** Make the same point concerning Chicagoans' connections to Southwest Florida in just one paragraph.

Part III: Why "Wordsmithing" Is Always the Last Step in Refinement

After you've checked on the alignment of a document, it is the right time to begin fine-tuning the document, or "wordsmithing," as mentioned earlier in this chapter. This method does have its merits. It's generally considered to be a useful tool, as it provides a helpful final step in making words and sentences more precise and, as a result, strengthens and clarifies the overall argument.

Despite the advantages of wordsmithing, checking on the overall clarity of the writing should take precedence over word choice.

The most important step in refinement is to check on the alignment of ideas between the sentences, paragraphs, and the title of a written piece.

Prioritizing alignment of ideas over wordsmithing also helps to counteract an unhelpful writing habit possessed by many people with perfectionist tendencies: wordsmithing while composing. Practically speaking, this is akin to a very unhealthy form of multitasking.

Composing should concentrate on the creation of an initial draft that will provide the basis for changes and improvements toward the latter stages of the writing process. When a writer composes, especially in the early stages of a paper, the first products created are always rough and somewhat misshapen. It's like being a sculptor who also has to make the clay or cut some marble as the basis of a sculpture *before* it can be shaped. There's no point in trying to perfect a piece of work (be it sculpting or writing) that has not yet taken on some recognizable form. So, if you become flustered about finding the perfect words in the first draft of the second paragraph, you will end up spending energy on a process that does not move an essay forward very much. Moreover, because wordsmithing early in the writing process can even become an obstacle to creating the raw material that is the main outcome of composing, it can truly become unproductive.

Conclusion: The Advantages of Making Sure That Composing and Refining Are Two Distinct Steps of the Writing Process

The key thing to remember about the distinction between composing and refining is that these two stages in writing have very different goals. Trial and error occur while composing, so refinement should occur *after* most of the trial-and-error stage has been completed.

When you successfully separate the composition stage from the refinement stage, refining a piece of writing can be extremely impactful in improving the flow of the argument as well as its clarity. Together, these help to maintain the reader's attention.

Clearly differentiating these steps also benefits writers. If you believe in your ability to refine your ideas after a first draft, then you can be more relaxed and exploratory while composing. These two steps, then, understood and used correctly together, are mutually supportive: better composition leads to more meaningful refinement, and the ability to refine helps to enable composition.

Review and Apply: Refinement

- Refine a document by making sure that sentences and paragraphs are clear and that the components of your argument relate to one another logically.
- Don't worry about refinement too early in the writing process.
- The first and most important step in refinement is to check on the alignment of ideas between the sentences, paragraphs, and the title or theme of a written piece.
- The second step of refinement is checking on the clarity of individual sentences, which is often undermined by the following: poor transitions between sentences, grammatical mistakes within a sentence, confusing passages of several sentences, and repetition of a previously stated idea.

- "Wordsmithing"—searching for the best word or phrase in certain important moments of a written piece—is the last step of refinement. Left to the end, wordsmithing can put some polish and shine on a document.

Part III

....

Advanced Concepts

Complex Applications and Implications of the One-Idea Rule

Chapter 7

Using the One-Idea Rule to Plan and Complete Research Projects

....

Part I: First, Really Understand Your Audience Before Embarking on Your Research Project

Research projects can be exciting as well as excruciating for writers. On one hand, delving into the details of a topic can be interesting, engaging, and rewarding. However, the breadth and depth of existing work on any topic can either scare writers into paralysis or draw them into so-called "rabbit holes" of very specialized topics that may obscure the main theme or goal of their research project.

Defining a topic and making it manageable are arguably the hardest and most crucial parts of any research project, be that a research paper on some aspect of the history of the Equal Rights

Amendment or a summary of a company's revenue for the previous fiscal year. Communicating findings clearly is the next priority. Both of these aspects of research projects are covered in detail in the first part of this chapter, which focuses on academic research papers. For the vast majority of people, research in an academic setting is a useful prelude to applying research to settings outside of school because the foundational skills for research in both contexts are almost identical.

But there is a major difference between academic and nonacademic contexts: the audiences for nonacademic research work can vary far more than for research papers in an academic setting. Whereas the audience of an academic paper is usually an instructor (who often "stands in" for the community of specialists within a discipline), nonacademic research projects (especially in professional settings) can easily range from very narrow to very broad—from a pointed assignment requested by a supervisor to marketing copy for a large advertising campaign. After aligning the scope of research and writing to the needs of an audience, writers can confidently apply the one-idea rule to complete any given assignment.

For nonacademic projects, then, writers must be much more aware of how the audience should influence the written "deliverable" they produce from their research. Assessing a particular audience well can help determine: (1) the amount of research that is required for the writer to understand a certain issue for that audience, and (2) the amount of detail that is appropriate to share with that audience. Misalignment between what the writer knows and what the audience can understand (or wants to understand) is a common problem associated with research projects. Symptoms of this misalignment include (among many others) overreliance on specialized jargon and delving too deeply into specifics.

Part II: Academic Research Papers: Why They're Assigned and How to Complete Them

To complete a research paper, writers usually gather information and develop an informed perspective on a topic based on published work, which usually appears in professional journals and publications. Then, they sometimes must present an argument or offer a strong point of view about that topic that references that published work. When writers begin to explore the potential depth and complexity of a research topic for school, they may feel overwhelmed by all the scholarship that has already been produced about it. "What have I got to say," they might ask, "that hasn't already been said?"

The one-idea rule can help steady your nerves in facing these kinds of layered assignments that feature your thoughts as well as the thoughts of others. Although there's a lot to keep track of while writing a research paper, the rule can help you manage that information efficiently in support of your argument. Remembering that every part of a well-written document should express only one idea, you can aim to use the title or thesis of your papers as a way to choose and align research that is pertinent to your arguments—and, perhaps more importantly, to keep less significant or extraneous information *out* of your papers. In other words, imagine yourself as an expert within the limited domain you define for yourself as the theme of your research work.* For all research projects, especially in academic settings, the one-idea rule might be slightly modified to be called the "one manageable idea" rule.

Once you find a feasible theme to shape your project, you can start composing as you would with any other paper with the help of the one-idea rule. Below, we will cover how the one-idea rule can help to execute the ideation, composition, and refinement stages of research papers.

Before embarking on this, we should note that instructors can have varied teaching goals in assigning research papers, which is important for writers to consider as they search for a theme to shape their work.

There are three different goals of assigning research papers, each of increasing complexity:

1. Have students learn more about a topic.
2. Make sure students support their ideas and claims with facts and arguments from reliable sources.
3. Have students practice constructing and defending an argument in the context of recent work and debates on a subject.

The first goal is often emphasized in high school research papers. For students who are just being introduced to research

---

* As will be discussed in the next chapter, the one-idea rule also gives beginners in any subject useful measures to judge all other writers, which consist of answering two questions: (1) Has this expert writer constructed an argument that conforms to the one-idea rule? (2) Has the writer made that argument clearly (in sentences, paragraphs, sections, and chapters) to the reader?

topics, this task can be a very effective learning tool. In this case, students often use research principally as sources of information—facts, figures, and quotations that help to create a fuller picture of a problem or an issue that the instructor or the student has chosen to explore. Requiring, for instance, five "outside sources" to be quoted or cited in a paper will help students learn a lot about a particular subject. In addition, they will start to become familiar with the challenges and questions that arise when performing research about any subject, such as "How do you know when a source is reliable?"

Instructors often add another layer of complexity to research papers by requiring students to support most of their major arguments by citing outside sources. This exercise requires writers to explore topics more deeply, which means moving from using outside sources mainly for illustrations and/or more details regarding certain ideas to employing outside sources to enter into current scholarly discussions about a specific topic.

In reading over research, writers learn that recent scholarship usually features debates and disagreements, not consensus. While we can look backward into any subject (physics, political science, dairy production, etc.) and assess the correct and incorrect beliefs within a profession or among a group of experts from the year 1923, for instance, scholarship done in the recent past and present features disagreements. That is because research on "cutting edge" topics usually progresses in many stages before a majority of experts agree that new claims about a topic are either true or useful.

The third goal for research papers is to place writers into conversation with a discipline's body of knowledge as it's being built. This is the most challenging kind of research paper and might more commonly take the form of an undergraduate thesis or work required for a master's degree or a doctorate. Below, we will apply the one-idea rule to an overview of completing the second kind of research paper (which most students reading this book will encounter in higher education and continuing adult education).

If you've completed research papers successfully before, much of the information in the remainder of this section will already be familiar to you. If so, skipping to Part III, which covers non-academic research papers and projects, may make more sense. However, if it's been a while since you've done a research project, this section will offer a useful review of fundamentals concerning (1) finding a manageable, interesting research topic, and (2) using the one-idea rule to efficiently share discoveries derived from research.

Many young writers are first introduced to research papers by writing about topics that are narrowly defined by instructors.* Prompts provide pathways of research and discovery that the writer knows are valuable to complete the assignment, and writers can gain a lot of focus that will push their work forward in the right direction—toward an apt "one idea"—by paying close attention to the word choice in a prompt. By providing a prompt, instructors allow writers to focus on learning how to search for information pertinent to a topic as well as how to integrate that information into their papers.

---

* Examples of a narrowly defined subject of a research paper could include scientific prompts such as "Describe the lives of bees over a calendar year" or topics in the humanities such as "What was the public and critical reception of Tolkien's *The Hobbit* when it was published in 1937?"

Later, when they move past the introductory level of a topic, writers are often asked to become increasingly independent in their work. The first crucial step in this process is to come up with original topics to research.

In becoming more autonomous in conducting research projects, writers may feel added pressure if they lack the guidance on research topics they may have received as beginners. Faced with the prospect of assignments that require more preparation and independent analysis, writers sometimes overreact in two contrasting ways. On one hand, this higher bar of performance can scare writers into feeling that their work has to be perfect (or close to perfect), which leads to overthinking their construction of sentences and paragraphs. On the other hand, some writers may just want to "get it all over with" and jump into writing without much preparation.

While broadly defined research topics can require more work than those that are narrowly defined, writers should take comfort knowing that the one-idea rule can greatly mitigate the new challenges posed by this kind of work. By using the one-idea rule's approach to creating documents (ideation-composition-refinement), writers can make the unfamiliar much more familiar and thus reduce a lot of the scariness of research papers with broadly defined topics.

Ideation for a Research Paper on Environmental Studies

Ideation is probably the hardest step for inexperienced writers of research papers because students begin by encountering what might seem like too much information and too many ideas. How can a beginner confidently start to make choices about which research to read concerning a complicated topic? What's worth reading, and what isn't? What is one to make of it all? And how does one eventually arrive at "one idea" to focus on after doing this research?

As mentioned above, coming up with a research topic independently is a more complicated task than answering a narrowly defined question. That is because these kinds of assignments often require writers to come up with an interesting and useful question to answer. To ask a useful question about some aspect of a discipline of study, in turn, requires a deeper understanding of a discipline than is required for a paper that responds to a prompt.

For new research paper topics that have little direction from an instructor, start with a hunch for a theme or interesting problem, and then use that hunch as a way to begin evaluating pertinent research. Once a narrower topic has been selected that piques the writer's interest, the writer has found a potential "one idea" to investigate.

The next step is to look for research that is pertinent to that idea. This can usually be found in "review articles" that are written by scholars in a field.* A review article focuses on summarizing

---

* There may be a little confusion in distinguishing between book reviews and review articles. While they are similar, each has a different focus. A book review focuses on one book and often places that book within a wider field of study. A review article focuses on the history of a wide field of study and places many books and articles within that field to assess their contributions. Review articles can be found by searching for terms and combining them with other keywords in an appropriate search engine. To find discussions on the study of tourism around the globe, for example, one could start with the terms "global," "tourism," and "review article." Not every topic has a review article dedicated to its specific contours, but some sort of review article will usually exist for a related topic and can be a good place to start.

and assessing work on a specific topic as well as finding patterns of inquiry and debate among all the pieces considered (mainly books and articles).* For professionals, this helps to describe promising avenues of their own future research. For novices, review articles reveal the major questions that frame and shape research about a topic. These questions can become the sources of a hypothesis or main idea that can be used to start a first draft of a research paper.

To demonstrate this ideation step by step, let's imagine a broad topic of a research paper in an environmental studies course. To give students freedom to survey possible topics on their own, the professor in this course can simply assign the following: "Write an eight- to ten-page research paper on a topic concerning environmental pollution that we have not covered in detail in this course. Use at least ten sources."

> *Starting with a hunch.* If you are interested in pollution issues related to plastic, for instance, you could begin your research by using a reliable search engine like Google Scholar. After entering the terms "plastics" and "pollution" in its search box, you could find three articles and a book bringing up related issues:
> - economic development and technology
> - eco-friendly bioplastic film

---

* Introductions to academic books written by experts in a field are like review articles because they usually explain why and how a book contributes to a field or discipline. Some academic books devote entire chapters to the review of a topic. Also, reviews of pertinent books on a topic in academic journals (like the *New England Quarterly*) will lay out popular lines of inquiry devoted to that topic. Reviews of work designed for a nonacademic audience, such as those found in the *New York Times Book Review*, can provide useful introductions to a topic for beginners.

- plastics pollution related to COVID-19
- marine plastics and politics

Looking for pertinent research related to the hunch. In addition to the four issues highlighted above, there are many other topics brought up in other related articles. To choose a path through this vast amount of research, you should seek out a topic that truly piques your interest so that you'll be motivated to find important scholarship related to that topic. The narrower the topic, the easier it is to find pertinent research and to assess the research's importance in its field.*

If the topic of marine plastics is of particular interest to you, a little searching for work related to that term yields an article with more than four hundred citations: "Plastics in the marine environment: the dark side of a modern gift."† Here's a very pertinent piece that offers a historical take on this topic; moreover, the research cited within this article will also be related to the topic of marine plastics and will provide more useful clues. Another recent article on the topic brings up a new term that could be important: "single-use plastics."‡

---

* The importance of a particular paper within a field of research is usually gauged by the number of times an article has been cited, except for articles that have been published relatively recently—say, within the past year or so. The reputation of an author within a field also provides a good clue about the value of a specific piece, but it is not a guarantee that any particular piece is strong or influential.

† Jort Hammer, Michiel H. S. Kraak, and John R. Parsons, "Plastics in the marine environment: The dark side of a modern gift," *Reviews of Environmental Contamination and Toxicology* 220 (2012): 1–44.

‡ Riley Schnurr et al., "Reducing marine pollution from single-use plastics (SUPs): A review," *Marine Pollution Bulletin* 137 (2018): 157–71, doi:10.1016/j.marpolbul.2018.10.001.

With these few steps, you've narrowed the topic from "environmental pollution" to "plastics pollution in the oceans" and have also found a number of possibly useful pieces of research and information that could contribute to an essay on the topic. Already, this originally broad question is becoming a more specific and manageable topic that a beginner might feel more able to address.*

Now that a narrower topic has been determined (e.g., plastics pollution in the ocean), the next step is to find a pertinent review of the scholarship. While a formal review article is always preferred at this stage, any recent article on a similar topic will situate itself to some extent within existing scholarship.

Going back to Google Scholar, you can now input terms that are closely related to this narrowed range of research: "marine pollution plastics review article." Doing so, a citation appears that seems to be highly regarded because it has been cited by other researchers almost four thousand times: "The pollution of the marine environment by plastic debris: a review."†

Upon closer examination of the article, you might also notice a publication date of 2002. Does that mean the article is not as current as it should be? The answer is yes and no. Yes, because the

---

* For beginners in any field, specificity of a topic or theme *always* makes research papers easier. While larger and more ambitious themes (e.g., how to end the use of plastics by 2050) can be even more inspiring (and inspiration is great fuel for writing), always be careful to calibrate your topic with the knowledge you bring to it along with the time you have to complete the corresponding assignment. Being inspired is great, of course, but finishing on time is even more important. If you don't have enough time to devote to topics of inspiration, some curiosity and interest will suffice.

† José Derraik, "The pollution of the marine environment by plastic debris: A review," *Marine Pollution Bulletin* 44, no. 9 (September 2002): 842–52, doi:10.1016/S0025-326X(02)00220-5.

research used for the paper assignment should not lean too heavily on an article that is twenty years old in this field, seeing that a lot of related work and discoveries must have been accomplished since 2002. At the same time, no, because the article's great popularity points to the fact that it is still being used. What this article must have done was to largely set the terms of debate in 2002 and, therefore, has since shaped many of the questions that researchers have been answering about marine plastics for the past two decades. (Looking up the author's more recent work may provide some updates for the 2002 article.)

There is an important caveat about reviewing research at this early stage of a research paper assignment: in general, one should begin the research process by skimming papers and articles while searching for the "one idea" focus of a research paper; otherwise, you risk wasting a lot of time and energy. Aware of your lack of familiarity with a subject, you may feel obliged to read all or most of the articles you first encounter in your research. This would be premature. Over the course of your reading, you may learn that your hunch has led to a dead end in a field of research for one of several reasons (e.g., new technology opened up more promising avenues of inquiry in recent years) or that the details of a topic are not as interesting as you first thought. Much of this information can be ascertained by skimming over pieces instead of reading them thoroughly.

In terms of the one-idea rule, this is "the stage of ideation that might be compared to the wide end of a funnel, when you gather as many options as you can" (see chapter four). For research papers (as opposed to personal essays), the important questions found in that funnel are largely determined by previous work on the topic. Even if a writer's aim is to create a new line of inquiry (rather than developing or improving on an older one), they must still explain why their new "funnel" is important and where it resides next to other main lines of inquiry.

The article about "The pollution of the marine environment by plastic debris" does, in fact, describe many research questions related to the problem of marine-plastics pollution. Subheadings of the article include "ingestion of plastics" by marine animals and the problems created by "plastic 'scrubbers.'" One of the last sections in the article is about "plastics pollution and legislation." For students who also have an interest in law, the material in this section could be perfect for their research papers. A passage in this article taken from another scholar in this field might provide some confirmation that this particular topic is important and worth their time: "no effort to conserve biological diversity is realistic outside the economics and public policies that drive the modern world."*

Having found a general topic that is both sufficiently narrow and interesting (marine single-use plastics and public policy), you can now begin to read pertinent research with much more attention and begin the process of composing. Further narrowing of the topic will occur once you discover an argument or angle that can be used to discuss the topic.

Composing for a Research Paper on Environmental Studies

Because writers embarking on a new subject of research are sometimes intimidated by the copious amounts of work they have to do before even writing their first sentence about that subject, they may

---

* Derraik, "The pollution of the marine environment by plastic debris," 848.

feel reluctant to assert their voice within their own work. In some extreme cases, writers hide behind scholarship by offering supporting evidence for every sentence they write. This results in blurring the focus of their research papers and elevating the research they've done above their own reasoning.

While supporting arguments with the work of experts in a field is key, making your own argument is just as important. To do this, remember to imagine yourself as an expert within the limited domain you've chosen as the theme of your research work. By defining that domain clearly, you can more easily "master" a limited set of materials and employ those materials primarily to support the claims you're making and elevate your voice. See how that voice emerges strongly in the opening paragraph of the final draft of this paper on plastics pollution:

What a Waste: The Unsustainability of Single-Use Plastics and How We Can Do Better

Of all the types of pollution that our society produces, plastics continue to prove to be one of the most challenging to deal with. Because plastics are very difficult, if not impossible, to recycle, simply discarding them has been the most common fate for any given plastic product.* Particularly wasteful are single-use plastics, which, as the name suggests, are only intended to be used once before being thrown away. Of the 400 million tons of plastic produced globally each year, 36 percent of it is single-use packaging.† Food containers, plastic wrappers, linings

---

* Travis P. Wagner, "Reducing single-use plastic shopping bags in the USA," *Waste Management* 70 (December 2017): 3–12, doi:10.1016/j.wasman.2017.09.003.

† "Beat Plastic Pollution," United Nations Environment Programme," accessed January 6, 2023, https://www.unep.org/interactives/beat-plastic-pollution/.

for cardboard and paper boxes, straws, and shopping bags are now predominantly composed of plastic and not meant to be reused.* So far, initiatives to reduce plastic consumption and waste have been mostly futile and have sometimes involved deceptive labeling around modified plastics that are supposedly biodegradable. In order to tackle the problem of plastic pollution, we must compel consumers to change their habits by instituting targeted bans and fees on single-use plastics, as well as find alternative materials for every plastic product possible.

In this paper, the writer eventually found their voice by making a clear statement of a central argument (the "one idea") in the final sentence. The title shows that the initial focus of the research on "marine plastics" shifted to the issue of "single-use plastics," a related topic that was first discovered during the ideation process. This is a normal adjustment that often occurs during the composition process (as discussed in chapter five). Writers are at liberty to adjust the focus of their writing during the composition process, but their final draft needs to offer one clear path for readers to follow.

In the opening paragraph, notice also that the scholarship acts as a buildup to the statement of the central idea, providing a useful preface to the writer's assertion of their argument on remedying (or "tackling") the problem of plastics pollution, an argument that seems focused and informed. While this thesis-statement sentence could have also been used more conventionally as the first sentence of the paragraph, its placement at the end acts like a culmination of the entire paragraph, thus adding a little tension to the narrative as

---

* João S. C. Viera et al., "On replacing single-use plastic with so-called biodegradable ones: The case with straws," *Environmental Science & Policy* 106 (April 2020): 177–81, doi:10.1016/j.envsci.2020.02.007.

the reader awaits the resolution of the troubling issues detailed in the preceding sentences.

Finally, note that the tone of the paper is clearly appropriate for a persuasive piece: not only does the writer aim to convince the reader of the urgency of plastic pollution, but they are also advocating for a solution or course of action that at least some readers will object to. Persuading this audience will require more focused discussion aimed at confronting counterarguments and changing minds by using appropriate evidence and logic.

Refinement for a Research Paper on Environmental Studies (Dealing with Research That Contradicts One's Thesis)

In a research paper, one of the major obstacles to promoting one's argument or main idea can be found in the conclusions of other researchers. Alternative viewpoints to one's thesis are almost certain to be publicly available, and they often pose real challenges to an argument's persuasiveness. Beginning writers might feel tempted to ignore or dismiss competing viewpoints and just focus on shoring up their own. But readers (especially instructors and bosses) are probably aware of those challenges and would be eager to hear how a writer might respond to some detractors, at least.

Writers should embrace this challenge rather than reluctantly give in to it. That is because meeting criticism head-on increases the credibility of one's argument by demonstrating its strength. Moreover, successfully dealing with select objections that pose the greatest difficulty to one's argument can reassure readers that the writer can probably also respond to lesser objections without much difficulty. Finally, if a reader is aware of some important objections that exist but remain unmentioned by the writer, that can seriously undermine the writer's credibility because it suggests that the writer may not be adequately familiar with the full scope of the issue they're addressing.

In the case of the topic of single-use plastics, one contending viewpoint focuses on plastic bags often used for shopping. If they were banned, some scholars maintain, adopting alternatives like paper bags and cloth bags would also add significant amounts of carbon into the atmosphere. In response, one researcher asserts that reducing plastic pollutants requires a cooperative effort among many sectors of society, not just a swapping out of one cause of pollution for another:

> [T]o address root causes of SUP [single-use plastics] use and mismanagement, governments need to improve waste management practices and introduce financial incentives to change behaviour of consumers, retailers and manufacturers, by enacting strong policies that push for a circular model of design and production of SUPs.*

While the debate between these two camps may continue long after the writer has turned in the assignment, dealing with an important contending view may satisfy at least some skeptical readers. This refinement for a research paper increases the writer's credibility, a key component of persuading readers that the argument is sound.

Research papers present a considerable challenge to inexperienced writers. Finding and maintaining one's voice in a crowded field of experts can be very difficult and intimidating. But when

---

* Schnurr et al., "Reducing marine pollution from single-use plastics (SUPs)."

instructors ask students to write a research paper, they usually don't intend for that paper to offer a mere summary of existing research. Instructors want to know what their students think about a certain subject, a subject that requires familiarity with other ideas and work in a discipline (i.e., research) to be worthwhile to investigate.

For students, the first thing that research papers do is familiarize them with the minimal requirements for an explanation or an argument (i.e., narrative styles used in expository or persuasive essays) to be taken seriously by an audience of experts. Furthermore, students learn about the requirements for evidence and explanation in any given discipline. The methodologies for a paper in history, law, or physics all may be rigorous, but they're rigorous in different ways.

Finally, research papers should teach the virtue of modesty by revealing the potential complexity of almost any research topic— from the history of Mexican textiles to the technical requirements to create the Webb telescope. Looking below the surface of almost any topic can reveal an impressive array of detail and depth that should put a writer on notice that mastering *any* topic requires a lot of work and persistence.

An interesting potential outcome of this modesty is remaining open to learning, to listening to others with different points of view. Building on this understanding, writers can begin work on any topic by first taking inventory of what they know and what they don't know and then defining the borders of each of those domains. Assessing this inventory is crucial in setting limits to a research project. Those limits show where writers can start directing their efforts to move beyond their current understanding of a particular discipline.

To ensure that their voices do emerge from the storehouse of existing research, beginners in any discipline should prioritize narrowing the field of research for an assignment as much as possible and carefully define the questions they want to answer in the ideation stage. If the research in that narrowed field is manageable, then they can apply the one-idea rule as they would with any other writing assignment. After trying this a few times, you should be able to gain confidence, allowing your thoughts more freedom to discover exciting new ideas and welcoming engagement with interesting controversies during refinement.

By adding your voice to complicated and important issues, you might eventually contribute to the collective knowledge of any discipline.

Part III: Nonacademic Research Projects

As mentioned in the introduction, all successful documents conform to the one-idea rule. But getting to that final version can vary greatly from task to task, depending on the kind of work you're producing. A final draft of most scientific papers, for instance, is often preceded by calculations and experiments that do not resemble most research projects in the humanities. A great challenge facing scientific writers concerns translating mathematical concepts and other highly specialized knowledge into words and sentences that a general audience can understand.

In addition to hard science, there are countless projects done outside of an educational context that can be seen as variations of academic research projects. For academic research, the audience is usually a community of experts in a specific discipline. For nonacademic research projects, readers can range from an expert audience of one (e.g., a boss) to an audience of millions in the general population (e.g., for a public service announcement). In other words, the size of the audience and its familiarity with a certain topic must both be taken into account when a writer chooses an appropriate "one idea" for a research project. Assessing the needs of a particular audience is the most significant variable that distinguishes academic from nonacademic research projects, and it requires careful consideration on a case-by-case basis.

In the examples that follow, we look at five very different nonacademic research projects with audiences ranging greatly in size. After assessing the audience's familiarity with a specific topic as well as its size, we will determine how to deliver that information in accordance with the audience's knowledge and interest in a research topic. Each example is broken down into three parts: the assignment, an audience assessment, and preparing the deliverable.

Assignment #1: At Work, Create a Report for Your Boss

Your boss wants you to prepare a report for her that compares revenues from this year's new product launch to the launch for a similar product from two years ago. She also asks you to offer some possible explanations concerning why the earlier product launch had higher revenues in the first six months after launch than those of the more recent launch.

Audience Assessment

Because the reader is very familiar with your domain of work, you can skip a lot of introductory explanations and focus on sophisticated or advanced concepts. In offering a number of possible explanations to a problem, detailed responses will be welcome, but you should be careful to be very organized in presenting your findings to avoid extraneous information and/or confusion caused by multiple, competing messages.

Preparing the Deliverable

The boss is asking for research that involves two tasks. In the first task, comparing revenues from two product launches, the "one idea" has been completely provided by the supervisor. The only modifications to that idea that you could make should concern questions about the meaning of the assignment. Once any ambiguities about the assignment have been resolved, the writing should proceed easily because it just focuses on providing data that is directly related to the question.

In the second task, your boss is asking you to offer possible explanations concerning the differences in revenues between the two product launches. For a writer following the one-idea rule, this assignment could seem difficult to accomplish. If a document offers multiple explanations based on the same data, then the resulting piece would be about many ideas, not one. Luckily, if your supervisor's intent is understood correctly, then the assignment can be executed with clarity.

Your supervisor would like you to get some thinking started on this issue so they can begin working on this problem with the head start of having considered at least some plausible explanations for the different revenue numbers. One way for you to provide these explanations is to begin with the analysis of the revenue numbers, followed by a series of very short "essays" of one or two paragraphs, each representing *one* plausible answer (each answer being one idea) to the revenue discrepancies.

Example:

Please provide some explanations concerning why unit sales for this year's new beach umbrella, "More Shades," were lower than the sales from a similar product we offered two years ago.

- US sales numbers from March to September 2020 for "The Shade," a large beach umbrella produced in three colors: yellow, blue, and green: **475,000 units**.
- US sales numbers from March to September 2022 for "More Shades," a medium-sized beach umbrella manufactured in multicolored variations: **300,000 units**.

Background information: "The Shade" was designed for vacationing in the COVID-19 era. Because families often stayed together in "pods" to vacation, a simple and sturdy large umbrella seemed well suited for a safe group escape to the outdoors on the beach. "More Shades" was made smaller in response to the transition to a reduction in overall COVID-19 restrictions on mobility and gatherings in 2022. We anticipated more people going out in smaller groups, even as individuals, to enjoy the beach.

Explanation #1:

Post-lockdown reversion to older vacationing habits was more rapid than we had anticipated. The strong sales of "The Shade" in 2020 seemed to indicate that many beachgoers would continue to explore outdoor options for leisure even after many COVID-19 restrictions were lifted. The smaller beach umbrella was created to accommodate increased freedom of choice for beachgoers who might now visit the coast in smaller groups or even alone. However, it seems that overall attendance at indoor events in the United States dramatically rose in popularity in 2022, making the beach a less central option for leisure activities.

Explanation #2:

Changes in umbrella color and décor detracted from the appeal of "More Shades." "More Shades" added smaller size and multicolor decorations to our beach umbrella offerings. These changes resulted from research that suggested we could expand the market to those breaking away from their safe "pods." These consumers who were no longer attached to a close group of family or friends would now buy umbrellas for fewer people and would express themselves in more varied ways (i.e., they would be attracted to more variations in color schemes). However, rising inflation dampened this demand for variation and influenced people toward safer products that can be used for many years. Although the designs of the two lines of umbrellas are equally sturdy, the multicolor schemes for "More Shades" made the umbrellas seem less practical and more delicate than consumers would have preferred, which was not anticipated.

Assignment #2: At Work, Share Information from Your Team with Another Team in Your Company

You are part of a team of software developers that is making updates to a website. You are asked to share and discuss a timeline of software updates to the website with another team whose work depends on the functionality of the website.

Audience Assessment

Communication among teams is a common and sometimes tricky process that happens often in a company or organization. When one person is summarizing the work of a team to an outside party, that summary usually has to be approved by some or all other members of that team to make sure it represents their work accurately. Then, the summary has to be carefully calibrated to satisfy the different needs of both teams: the "home" team that you are part of and the "away" team that is asking for information. This is quite a challenge for using the one-idea rule because the rule is ideally applied for only one audience at a time.

Preparing the Deliverable

In addressing members of your own team, you can take some concepts and details for granted in communication because you have been collaborating consistently on similar work; therefore, the one idea that shapes any written updates can focus on relatively subtle or complicated concepts.

Communication to people on other teams, however, has to be more carefully calibrated than communication with your own team. You need to determine what the other team needs to know to work with your team efficiently and explain information clearly to fill any gaps in their knowledge. Ultimately, the one idea that you use to guide internal and external communication for this task should be very similar, but the explanations required for the external team will require more steps than you would take for your teammates; therefore, you need to filter out information that is not clearly connected to the theme of your communication because of the extra time you will need to take to explain some details of your work to outsiders.

This filtering occurs in part for political reasons because the team you work on may not want to reveal internal problems or weaknesses to other parts of the company. But the filtering also occurs to avoid communication problems among teams and within a company. Sharing information about projects in the planning stage can create unwanted tension and confusion. In the scenario above, perhaps your team that oversees maintaining your company's website is now considering making some new or additional changes to the website that could impact the work of other teams. If those changes are merely speculative and not close to being decided, then sharing information about them could cause needless anxiety and resistance from other parts of the company. This gaffe could result in spending valuable time conducting follow-up communication assuring others that no final decisions have yet been made (known also as "damage control"). Even if you do a good job explaining your mistake, your team may now seem less trustworthy to outsiders.

Using the one-idea rule can help to create helpful communication filters by concentrating the components of written and verbal statements on conveying just *one* clear message. In the above example, the theme of sharing news about recent software updates to a website is not supported by adding speculations about future major changes to the website.

Example:
Share programming updates about changes to how consumers purchase products on a retail website *from* your "home" team of programmers *to* an "away" team in charge of kitchen-appliance sales.

Background information: Your team of programmers has been working on fixing small problems that consumers have encountered in completing purchases on your website. As your team has been tending to these issues, you have found that the best solution would be to overhaul this buying process by making it easy for consumers to buy anything they see on the site instantly upon finding it (with just "one click" of the mouse). While experiments with this process have been promising, your team is not close to finalizing a methodology for it.

Message from programming team to kitchen-retail team about website updates:

The latest updates to the website have focused on two issues: making credit-card information easier to input, and facilitating the review of items in a shopping cart right before the consumer purchases those items.

- For the credit cards, we've placed the "input" and "update" buttons for credit-card information adjacent to one another. We've also added text to further clarify each respective action to "input new card" and "update existing card," which received strong positive responses in user testing and surveys. This will help to reduce confusion concerning these different buttons.

- For the review of items in a shopping cart, we aimed to make all the items easier to scan at one glance by compressing their presentation on the checkout page. Now, consumers will first see only the name of each item, with details available by clicking the item's name. This responds to research showing a correlation between an increase in purchases and the ability of consumers to scan more items at a glance.

We are continuing to experiment with other ways to improve user experience in purchasing items on the website, and we will provide updates when we have useful information to share.

Assignment #3: Write a Single Set of Directions on How to Put Together a Table Being Sold by an International Company

You are told to create a single set of instructions to put together a table that is being sold to customers who span the globe and speak many different languages. The company does not want to spend time translating the directions into multiple languages. Ultimately, the directions will represent the sequential steps required to assemble the table in numbers and pictures. This is the goal or "one idea" of the assignment.

Audience Assessment

In this case, while the goal is to create instructions that are very simple to understand, assessing the audience's needs is more complicated. First, the audience is both homogeneous and diverse. While everybody reading these instructions has a common interest in putting a particular table together, their experience in assembling furniture and their spoken languages are very diverse. To ensure that most consumers can assemble the table successfully, the writer should have a generic consumer/reader in mind whose experience in assembling furniture is minimal.

Preparing the Deliverable

To create a document that is clear and simple for customers to follow without words will require several preceding steps that will involve some sophisticated research reports. First, if this is your first time creating a generic set of directions for an international audience, you will have to research best practices for communicating through pictures. Second, you must learn (through data and reports probably provided by another team in the company) what are the necessary steps in the process of putting together the table.

Then, and most importantly, you should write out all the steps for yourself as a kind of verbal blueprint for ultimately creating the visual instructions. This detail is necessary long before any pictures are created because pictures summarize or highlight the most important steps in the process. But that summary can only be determined after making sure all the necessary aspects of putting the table together are explained clearly. When that complete description is finished, you can then determine how best to represent the essential parts of the furniture assembly through a series of pictures.

For an example, consider IKEA's assembly instruction manual for its KIVIK sofa.* First, readers are told to assemble the couch with the help of others and are shown the difference between an unsafe basis for assembling the couch (e.g., on a bare floor) and a safe basis (e.g., on a floor covered with a rug or carpet to prevent slipping or damage). Second, there are clear instructions to call an IKEA office to answer questions or to clear up confusion about the assembly. With these fundamental issues now covered, the reader can proceed with the more complicated details to fulfill the goal of the instructions, which is to make a sofa.

---

* The PDF of these instructions can be found in the "Assembly & documents" section (within the "Product details" tab) for the IKEA KIVIK sofa: https://www.ikea.com/us /en/p/kivik-sectional-4-seat-with-chaise-grann-bomstad-black-s99443193/, accessed January 6, 2023.

Assignment #4: Prepare a White Paper on a New Fire-Alarm System Sold to Hotels and Restaurants

Your company has just developed a new fire-alarm system that has made improvements in reducing false alarms resulting from smoke generated in kitchens. You're told to prepare a white paper about the product to be distributed mainly at trade shows.

Audience Assessment

In stark contrast to the furniture-construction manual discussed above, white papers usually have a more well-defined reader or user and prominently feature and discuss research done for those readers. While white papers are designed to help market a product, they are not flashy like TV ads. Instead, they use research to help explain the advantages of a product or service to buyers who need to know about important trends in their industry *or* how a product works and what problems it solves. The likely audience for this new fire-alarm system would be buyers representing hotels or restaurant chains who may decrease their costs and increase customer satisfaction significantly by reducing false alarms at their establishments.

Preparing the Deliverable

White papers resemble research papers and sometimes include references to outside sources in footnotes. The ultimate goal of a white paper is, of course, to increase sales for a company, but this is often done in an indirect way. White papers aim to raise the reputation of the authorial company, often by offering trustworthy insights based on research about the needs of an industry that might be hard to find from another source.

Special care in formulating a title may help to maintain this difficult balance between providing reliable general information and advocating for a particular company, which is a subtle idea to convey. This task might be aided by the focused goal of the white paper to quietly portray the company in the best light.

In the case of creating the "one idea" for a white paper about this fire-alarm company, you could choose to focus on broad industry themes, in which the company plays a supporting role, or more specific themes that clearly focus on the company's product. Titles that focus on wider industry issues could include "Health and Safety Concerns for the Restaurant Trade Since COVID-19" or "Networked Sensor Technology and Opportunities for Improvement in Alarm Systems." An example of this kind of white paper was produced by a financial company that published a document providing some answers to the question "Are equities overvalued?"*

Titles that focus on the fire-alarm product could include "First-Notice Alarm Systems: Optimizing New Technology to Meet Stringent Safety and Compliance Standards" or "Best Practices for Installing and Maintaining the New Generation of First-Notice Alarms." An example of this kind of white paper was created by Hitachi to explain some of the complicated details concerning how to use its electronic platform: "Hitachi Content Platform Architecture Fundamentals."†

---

* See HSBC Global Asset Management, "Are Equities Overvalued? Taking an Active Approach to Asset Allocation," PDF file, accessed January 6, 2023, http:// www.frinfo.assetmanagement.hsbc.com/inews---publications/190_amfr_amch_wp _equityovervalued_04-2016_en.pdf.
† "Hitachi Content Platform Architecture Fundamentals," June 2020, accessed January 6, 2023, https://www.hitachivantara.com/en-us/pdf/white-paper/content-platform -architecture-fundamentals-whitepaper.pdf.

Assignment #5: Creating an Announcement for the General Public—Description of an Amendment to the Massachusetts State Constitution, November 2022

Imagine you work for the Office of the Secretary of State. You have been asked to write a first draft of the description of a ballot initiative that proposes to raise taxes by 4 percent on incomes over $1 million. The audience is the entire voting population of Massachusetts.*

Audience Assessment

This is probably one of the most diverse and broad audiences one might have to write for: all the adult citizens in a state. In addition, as a representative of the state, you cannot appear to favor any argument about the proposed amendment or any particular segment of that population.

Preparing the Deliverable

The main challenge in this research project is to find a "one idea" that's suitable for an incredibly diverse audience. The challenge is increased by the fact that the state cannot present any research findings as support for an argument. As a result, the "one idea" for this text cannot put forward an opinion. Instead, it has to be seen as providing sufficient and neutral information for the readers to make

---

* "Question 1: Proposed Amendment to the Constitution: Additional Tax on Income Over One Million Dollars," Secretary of the Commonwealth of Massachusetts website, accessed January 6, 2023, https://www.sec.state.ma.us/ele/ele22/information-for-voters -22/quest_1.htm.

up their own minds and come to their own opinions.* For this task, a suitable implied title could be as follows: "A clear description of a proposed amendment to the constitution and explanations of some possible financial outcomes."

As it appears on the Massachusetts Secretary of State's website, the text presenting this information does attempt to present enough information for readers to develop an opinion:

- **A clear description of the proposed amendment.** This is accomplished by foregrounding a summary of the amendment, which is written in everyday language instead of more formal legal terms. In addition, a link to the full text of the amendment is placed just underneath the summary.
- **Explanations of possible outcomes**. An effective tactic to present opinions about the amendment without appearing opinionated is to include arguments from public interest groups representing both supporting and dissenting views. These are included at the bottom of the web page. These views feature research and analysis that support the differing opinions.

The only research presented by the state concerns a "statement of fiscal consequences" that broadly outlines the impact of the law on some taxpayers and on generating new revenues, adding the caveat that "annual revenue generated by the surtax will vary significantly and unpredictably from year to year."

---

* In presenting information this way, the text about the amendment resembles the writing style of business cases that present information used as the basis for a classroom debate about a business decision.

Conclusion: Demonstrating Fairness to Your Audience in Research Projects

Collectively, all the examples of research projects in this chapter demonstrate how important it is for writers to be sensitive to the interests and knowledge of their audience. Discussing the topic of cell division in biology with a class of tenth-graders, for instance, requires a completely different approach than that for discussing the topic with graduate students pursuing a PhD. Fundamentally, it's the same topic, but the research required and the appropriate presentation and discussion of the topic must vary greatly according to each audience's respective understanding of biology.

Varying the message according to the audience brings up an interesting complication: ultimately, there is no single correct way to tell a story or construct a narrative. There are, instead, many different ways that are calibrated not only to the knowledge of the audience but also to the goals of the author or writer.

But if this is the case, then one may wonder: If there is no one right way to tell a story based on research and evidence, does that mean that all stories or arguments about a topic are potentially true? The answer is no. While the combination of authorial goals and audience knowledge can create many variations concerning a story, there are limits to what is persuasive and what is not in a research project. That is where research and its presentation become so vitally important.

For readers who may disagree with the "one idea" a writer is proposing, evidence is often crucial because it points to proof in the world outside the opinion of the writer. If a writer wants to show, for instance, that food prices are rising, then tracking the average price of eggs or milk over the past two years could help to convince a skeptical reader. The quality of that evidence is also crucial for seeming reasonable. There is a great difference, for instance, between gathering evidence from a professional trade group in the food industry compared to evidence from your local grocer. If your argument is based mainly on the latter source, it's bound to seem thin and unconvincing to an informed audience.

If writers manage to gather evidence from reliable sources, they still must present the information in a convincing way. In addition to constructing a logical argument, writers can gain the trust of their readers by demonstrating fairness in the treatment of the evidence, which means purposely *not* avoiding facts and ideas that challenge the writer's point of view. The easiest way for writers to show that they are fairly discussing research is to employ *transparency* in one's writing. This requires writers to be open and honest about how they've arrived at a conclusion. Writers of research projects gain credibility by supplying references of all the sources they use and some kind of description of their methodology for gathering evidence. Freely sharing research methods and research findings supplies a common ground that allows people to come together to disagree productively about similar evidence related to important issues.

Review and Apply: Research Projects

- For research assignments, the one-idea rule might be slightly modified to be called the "one manageable idea" rule.

- The amount of research that exists in most professional domains can be intimidating, but limiting the scope of your research can make it more manageable.
- For nonacademic writing, think carefully about the particular audience being addressed and calibrate the discussion of your research to that audience's interest and familiarity with a given topic.
- Imagine yourself as an expert within the limited domain that you have defined for yourself as the theme of your research work.
- If a topic of a research project is specified by an instructor, analyze the prompt for clues about the possible shape of your final draft—the "one idea" you can pursue.
- For more open-ended research without a narrowly defined topic, you'll have to do more work to define a manageable field of inquiry.
  - First, start with a hunch for a theme or issue and use that hunch as a way to start mining available research for a potential "one idea" to investigate further.
  - Find research related to your "one idea" by reading review articles that reveal the major questions around certain topics.
- Once the research question has been defined and restricted to a manageable scope, then you can employ the one-idea rule to complete the writing work.

Chapter 8

Evaluating Writing

....

Part I: Writing from the Reader's Point of View

So far, this book has focused on looking at essays and other kinds of documents mainly from the writer's point of view. But over the course of their careers as students, workers, and members of their communities, writers should become increasingly considerate of the reader's point of view because they need to be conscious of how readers receive their work. This shouldn't be done obsessively, of course, because that can discourage writers from exploring issues with openness and curiosity in developing their own voices. But as writers grow in their abilities, reader reception should become increasingly important in their minds as a means of improving their work—for what's the use of a good idea if it isn't expressed clearly and persuasively to its audience?

There is another useful aspect of looking at writing from the reader's point of view: good writers are also good (and engaged) readers. If a writer is going to discuss any topic that might be of some public interest, that discussion must be preceded by reading that familiarizes the writer with the major questions and issues related to that topic. Young writers in particular need to practice seeing themselves as worthy participants in matters of public debate. One way to move from spectator to participant in these matters is to develop a dependable approach to assessing the strengths and weaknesses of any piece of writing. The effectiveness of any document can be judged—at least in part—by how well it conforms to the one-idea rule.

Part II: How the Form and Content of a Document Support Its "One Idea"

While the one-idea rule provides writers with a useful approach to constructing a document from the very beginning of composition, readers can't be sure of knowing what a text's "one idea" is right away when they begin reading. That's because the reader usually needs some time to assess whether a document is effective in expressing and/or supporting that "one idea."

Before reaching that judgment, the reader encounters two supporting pillars of the theme or main idea of a document: the *form* and the *content* of the writing. "Form" usually refers to the architecture of a document: its overall logical flow from topic to topic, the clear expression of smaller ideas from sentence to sentence, and the reliability of supporting sources. "Content" usually refers to the details concerning the topic being explored, including the originality of the topic (either in the selection of the topic or in its treatment). To be believable and interesting, an argument must have both sound form and good content.

Reference books like dictionaries or encyclopedias combine strong form with clear content. Of course, they don't tell one story or narrative (as many documents do), but they often succeed in making a wide variety of information manageable to the reader. Successful reference books accomplish this through three characteristics. First, they clearly define the parameters of the book's scope (their "one idea") with titles like "The Encyclopedia of Agriculture" or "An Encyclopedia of Pharmacology." Secondly, most reference books organize the presentation of material by listing subjects in alphabetical order, which makes it easy for a reader to sift through vast amounts of information quickly.

While this overall format—or form, for our purposes—for reference books has become commonplace and does not require too much thought for an author or a managing editor to consider, the creation of narratives for individual entries (the content) must be undertaken with much more care. One of the promises of the form of reference books is that readers can quickly learn about the most important aspects of any topic within the allotted space of a single entry. To fulfill that promise, then, writers of these entries must have a very clearly (and often narrowly) defined "one idea" to shape the book's content, entry by entry.

Understanding how form can contribute to or detract from the clear communication of an idea or theme of a narrative might be most easily illustrated by analyzing the form of a live presentation. In contrast to a stand-alone text (like a magazine article) whose form is principally expressed through the written word, the form of an oral presentation often is presented through three kinds of "media" (or vehicles of communication): text, illustrations, and verbal communication. Learning how to manage these media types to support one idea clearly can be challenging.

One typical problem with form in presentations occurs when the audience is asked to understand messages from two or more kinds of media simultaneously (thus being forced to evaluate more than one idea at the same time). The most typical instance of this occurs when the audience is presented a slide featuring lots of text that they are implicitly invited to read while the presenter is speaking. Although slides like these offer the presenter a quick and convenient way to cover many details about a topic, this method of conveying information does not help the audience. Because the audience is being asked to listen and read simultaneously, one can be certain that either the verbal message or the written messages will not be fully understood. Oftentimes, neither is successfully conveyed in this kind of presentation, each undercutting the other as they vie for the attention of the audience.

A helpful practice in maintaining a strong form for presentations is to offer audiences some outline of the presentation's main points in the introductory section. This outline conveys the overall architecture of a document to the audience, one important idea at a time. In contrast, readers of relatively brief written documents do not usually need a preliminary outline because they can acquaint themselves quickly with the contents of a document simply by glancing over its pages. By doing so, they get a preview of the length of the discussion as well as other telling details, such as the relative complexity of the document (e.g., does it feature a lot of sophisticated research?) and whether the document has illustrations to support its argument. For an audience of a presentation, an outline or overview assures listeners that the presentation will follow a logical form, which helps them to trust the presenter's judgment as they are guided through a subject. It also assures the audience that the presenter will probably not ramble by discussing multiple contending ideas instead of just focusing on one.

In the relationship between form and content, one is often more dominant than the other. In some cases, form plays a decisive role in shaping content. The five-paragraph essay and the standard format for presenting information in a scientific journal both place strong constraints on the creativity a writer can employ in presenting content. The reason for these constraints is to compensate for some possible shortcomings in the development of content by the writer. In the case of the five-paragraph essay, writers are typically inexperienced and might find organizing content in a logical flow to be challenging. In the case of scientific journals, summarizing the methods and results of a complex scientific study could easily overwhelm writers whose primary domain of expertise is often *not* writing.

In other cases, content more clearly shapes form. In the case of writing about events or steps unfolding in a sequential manner, the content (e.g., details and explanations related to the central idea of that document) is presented in a way that conforms to the subject matter being discussed. The chronological and prioritization frameworks provide examples of the "self-explanatory" power of some content. The ordering of content in these kinds of frameworks is vital and doesn't allow for many variations. A sequence like a series of steps in a recipe, an instruction manual, or the biography of an individual usually must be written in a way that keeps the sequence constantly visible and understandable to the reader. For example, this book announces at the outset that it is shaped by a prioritization framework moving from basic to advanced discussions. This discussion on form and content might be hard to understand if it were placed at the beginning because it requires some familiarity with the one-idea rule and related concepts as a prerequisite.

While narratives shaped by a chronology may seem to be highly ordered and predictable at first glance, this predictability can provide a reliable foundation from which writers can launch highly creative works. Stories featuring travel of some sort (often called stories about a "road trip") have a built-in chronological framework, following characters from venue to venue, usually on a series of adventures. *Don Quixote* follows its titular character roaming the countryside seeking wrongs to right to fulfill his destiny as a knight. Epics like *The Odyssey* and *The Divine Comedy* are "road trips" with supernatural elements encountered by the main character. Many original movies use the road trip to organize the storytelling—from *It Happened One Night* (1934) to *Rain Man* (1988) to *Thelma & Louise* (1991).

A finer balance between form and content exists in documents with tentative findings or with multiple parts that do not need to be too logically connected. The Q&A framework discussed earlier, for instance, only promises a series of questions and answers, an architecture that does not add much to the understanding of the content except its most salient characteristic, which is that it is not yet entirely understood by the writer. Theater programs distributed during live performances (many theaters in the United States employ playbills) provide a similar example of a balance between somewhat loose form and content. Playbills orient audiences to some of the details concerning a performance. Also, they often serve to promote the theater as well by advertising future performances, soliciting contributions, and providing background information on actors and the theater's administrators. The sequence of these sections does not have to follow a strict format. Because readers are probably already interested in the theater (evidenced by their attendance), the writer or editor of the playbill doesn't have to be too careful about sequencing materials in the document with a "one idea" that is very broad: people, news, and events related to a particular theater.

In documents shaped by some sort of story or narrative (which is an essential part of expository and argumentative pieces), readers are constantly assessing both form and content, whether or not they are doing so deliberately. Determining the quality of form and content implicitly answers the first question every reader poses before reviewing a new document: Is this worth my time? By doing this assessment deliberately, readers can elevate themselves so they can see eye to eye with experts in many domains and have some useful criteria with which to judge the writing of those experts (with the important caveat of increasing their modesty in proportion to the sophistication and specialization of a topic addressed in a particular document).

A similar process occurs when high school and college instructors assess and grade written documents of their students. An "A" paper usually has superior form and content, while an "F" paper has neither. The grades in between those extremes represent various mixtures of form and content that are on their way to "superior" but have not quite arrived there. Because each individual has particular strengths and preferences as a writer, the proportions of those mixtures can vary from person to person; likewise, judging those mixtures can also vary a bit from reader to reader.*

---

* For those who know baseball, umpires calling balls and strikes provide a useful parallel to how the teaching profession may judge writing. Instances arise when the same close pitch on the edge of the strike zone may be called a strike by one umpire and a ball by another. Both pitchers and batters during a baseball game try to assess the "grading" tendencies of umpires and make adjustments. If an umpire consistently calls strikes for pitches thrown slightly above the strike zone, for instance, most of the baseball players will recalibrate their expectations (albeit, perhaps, reluctantly). While variations on "grading" in a baseball game are tolerated, inconsistency in following a given variation during a particular game can create controversy and anger among players and fans. The same goes for grading papers. Inconsistency between instructors can seem idiosyncratic but tolerable; inconsistency demonstrated by a single instructor implies either unfairness or incompetence.

Usually, the quality of form and content in a document are roughly equivalent: the qualities in one aspect generally also shape the other. For instance, if a document has poor form, the idea that form is carrying (or conveying) will probably not be clearly or fully expressed, even though it might have great potential.

The connection between the one-idea rule and form and content is that the rule is related to both. The rule acts as a bridge between form and content and also suggests how these two aspects of a document interact productively. The "idea" part of the one-idea rule draws the writer's attention to the importance of the topic (or content) of a paper. At the same time, the emphasis on expressing only *one* idea at a time is a constant reminder to the writer to communicate as clearly and directly as possible (in other words, to have good form). In trying to create simple and direct expressions of their ideas, writers almost immediately begin to make fewer mistakes in form.

The one-idea rule implicitly influences writers to make sound choices about form and content—choices that decrease the instances of tangled prose and weak narrative arcs. As we saw in the discussion of *Holistic Health for Adolescents* in the introduction, exploring *only* one major idea in any written document will encourage writers to find ways to connect that one idea to all the parts of the document that follow. Likewise, knowing that sentences, paragraphs, and sections of a document should each be dedicated to one major idea helps to prevent the narrative from fragmenting into side issues that could stray from that "one idea." For example, the very tightly focused titles of most of the book's chapters (like "Stress," "Fatigue," and "Low Mood") guard against including loosely related topics (like "increasing noise pollution in urban areas") that don't clearly promote the book's main theme: understanding therapies related to *holistic health for adolescents*.

Of course, it can be a bit intimidating for beginning writers to worry about both form and content. While the two need to work together, they are different, and it might seem difficult to deal with both simultaneously. My advice is to try to articulate the ideas/content clearly first. As discussed earlier, writing with a syntax that feels comfortable usually produces sentences that are clear and understandable. Once an idea is articulated, it can always be improved at a later time (in terms of either form or content). But without an idea, a writer has nothing to work with.

Part III: Evaluating Writing: Examples

We can use two extreme (and rare) examples to illustrate vividly how the quality of a document can be affected by either its form or its content.

Ineffective Paper #1: Interesting Content with Poor Form

Starting an essay with a clear and arresting sentence is very promising, but that promise may lose its potential without focused discussion and support. As an example of this lost potential, let's look at a sample opening paragraph responding to the question (or prompt) concerning how to satisfy energy needs in the future:

Energy is mass times the speed of light squared. Energy problems we are facing now can be solved with this understanding. Alternatives to current ways of collecting, distributing, and consuming energy can be both sustaining to the environment and supportive of the need to create new job opportunities. What we need now is a comprehensive vision of a new energy world, so we know where best to apply that understanding.

"Energy is mass times the speed of light squared" is certainly an intriguing opening sentence and could be the main idea for the essay; however, after that idea is expressed, the writer then must start to explain what aspects of this concept are important with some explanation, details, and/or supporting evidence.

However, if the writer's next sentence declares something equally bold and arresting, such as "Energy problems we are facing now can be solved with this understanding," most readers will probably be lost. Would readers at this point really come to the same "understanding" that is mentioned but not really explained by the writer? Without adequate support or discussion of the first sentence, the second sentence takes many logical steps ahead in a potential (yet undefined) argument. In terms of the one-idea rule, the second sentence seems to represent a second possible main idea for the essay—a fatal flaw.

The bold opening sentence requires that the writer give some time and attention to its implications, making sure that readers understand which aspects of that scientific formula relate to energy production or consumption. Unfortunately, the writer skips that step and seems to assume that readers share the writer's understanding of these subtle connections. While the essay began with a compelling insight that could lead to some other intriguing ideas, as a whole it ends up being confusing because it really presents two or more ideas that contend equally for the reader's attention; therefore, in terms of the one-idea rule, it is ineffective.

Ineffective Paper #2: Poor Content with Good Form

The opposite extreme from the essay above could be a short essay with an obvious topic that doesn't require much explanation or supporting information. Topic sentences like "People sweat on hot days" or "My sister is tall" open the door to uninviting or uninteresting essays:

> People sweat on hot days. Heat from the sun raises body temperature for people, and the body needs to have some ways to help people cool down. If there is no pool or pond close by, the next best thing is sweat. The sun's heat can be very difficult in the summer, when temperatures rise the most during the year. Most of the heat stroke and other problems related to heat for people occur when cooling from sweat is not enough to keep the body temperature down. So, it's important to be careful to keep an eye on your body temperature on hot days.

No matter how clearly the supporting arguments are written, the main point still isn't worthy of much of the reader's attention. A weak thesis also often forces the writer to include supporting points that can be trivial because they function mainly to fill space rather than to explain an interesting concept.

While both of these essays were generally ineffective, they did have some strengths according to the one-idea rule. The first example presented some related ideas (although not well organized) concerning an intriguing theme; the second essay's focus on a simple idea and the clarity of the sentences made it easy to read (while still not being very interesting).

Now, let's look at some of the characteristics of an average essay that has good but not outstanding qualities.

Above all, the foundation for any good paper is based on the clarity of the writing. An average idea, clearly expressed, is at least understandable. Readers may not remember this kind of essay a week or two after they've read it, but they won't be lost or confused while reading it. For instance, an essay may be technically proficient and have no mistakes in its grammar, but if its ideas lack extra insight, depth, or originality, it won't make a strong impression on the reader. Take this example of an essay that opens with a commentary about Charles Lindbergh:

> Heroes don't always seem to act heroically. Take the life of Charles Lindbergh, for example. He was a pioneering American aviator who was the first person to fly nonstop across the Atlantic Ocean. While he was an instant national hero after his amazing transatlantic journey in 1927, he later was suspected of being sympathetic to Nazi Germany because of his vocal opposition to US involvement in World War II. His problems in the public eye are typical of the lives of many celebrities who often seem to lead paradoxical double lives.

While the opening of the paragraph begins with a paradox that could grab a reader's interest, the thesis sentence at the end doesn't promise a deeper analysis than, perhaps, noticing this paradox in the lives of many celebrities over time.

The essay could have received a boost if the thesis focused on a question that required further analysis beyond finding different examples of "paradoxical double lives." Imagine the possibilities opened up by this ending to the paragraph:

> Celebrities like Lindbergh are often victims of a public that always craves exciting stories from them. Celebrities not only entertain; they also become entertainment. If the positive "story line" of a well-known person grows boring, the public usually enjoys following a sinister turn. This essay will try to explain why the public's love–hate relationship with celebrities has been a staple of American cultural life for decades.

Conclusion: What Separates Good Writing from Great Writing?

What are the characteristics of the best documents, especially in regard to essays? The short answer is that they usually build from the solid basics—good form and interesting content that are well calibrated—and add a dose of originality in their insights and flair in the writing. And since content and form are mutually supportive, a great idea can help inspire good writing technique, just as strong writing ability can help develop a good idea into a great one. In other words, the original themes of the most successful kinds of papers have been used to align supporting content that is expressed through logical structure and clear sentences. Strong writers do this well enough so that most of their readers end up surprised and delighted by many of their work's findings and turns of phrase.

Review and Apply:
Evaluating Writing

- Being a good reader is a fundamental component of being a good writer.
- Ultimately, the effectiveness of any document can be judged by how well it conforms to the one-idea rule, but it takes a little time for a reader to be able to assess whether a document is effective in expressing and/or supporting its main idea.
- Before reaching that judgment, the reader encounters two supporting pillars of the theme or main idea of a document: the *form* and the *content* of the writing.
  - "Form" usually refers to the architecture of a document.
  - "Content" usually refers to the details concerning the topic being explored.
- To be believable and interesting, an argument or main idea must offer both sound form and good content.

Chapter 9

The Conclusion Paradox: The Ending as a Bridge to a New Idea

....

Part I: The Difficulty of Conclusions

In the late 1970s, I read a very funny faux writing primer published by *National Lampoon* called "How to Write Good." It took up the thorny issue of how to end a narrative (in this case, it was a piece of short fiction). Appropriately, this discussion about endings appears in the beginning of the essay:

> All too often, the budding author finds that his tale has run its course and yet he sees no way to satisfactorily end it, or, in literary parlance, "wrap it up." Observe how easily I resolve this problem: "Suddenly, everyone was run over by a truck." -the end-
> . . . You'll be surprised at how many different settings and situations this ending applies to. For instance, if you were writing a story about ants, it would end "Suddenly, everyone was

run over by a centipede." In fact, this is the only ending you ever need use.*

Ending a narrative has its unique challenges, and it can commonly cause frustration for writers approaching the end of an effortful task. Some writers may say to themselves that if they have sought to prove a point or solve a problem and have done so successfully in an argument supported by logic and evidence, then a conclusion may seem a little superfluous—a formality that takes time but adds little value.

In contrast, some documents end quite emphatically with a culminating "call to action." This occurs in all sorts of written pieces that focus on persuading readers to do something in the immediate future. This encouragement can cover a range of activities. A poster announcing a political rally could exhort readers to "meet at the city hall tomorrow at 1 p.m." Similarly, an advertisement or an email could ask readers to buy something or sign up for a subscription.

According to many writing experts, conclusions in essays and similar kinds of pieces usually function as a final persuasive push, reminding the reader of the argument's main points and perhaps adding a little spice (like a quotation) or a slightly pleasing addition (like a humorous observation). This also helps the narrative come to a little crescendo that is intended to satisfy reader expectations by signaling that "this is the end." Some also advise that new ideas should not be inserted at the end, except to suggest other possibilities for further inquiry or research.

---

* Michael O'Donoghue, "How to Write Good," in *Humor Me: An Anthology of Funny Contemporary Writing*, ed. Ian Frazier (Seattle: Ecco, 2010): 284–95. This article originally appeared in the *National Lampoon* of March 1971.

Part II: Something Might Be Lacking in the Way Many Conclusions Are Constructed

"Summing up" generally describes what the conclusions of most written documents are doing, and this approach can work well. But there are a few drawbacks to this method, which are made clear with the one-idea rule.

- While every component of a well-written document should express only one idea, repetition of an idea that occurred previously in that document is generally ineffective. Arguments in an expository or argumentative essay should usually move forward as a series of related but discrete ideas supporting the main theme.
- Ending with a summary can become formulaic—an ending just like so many others readers have seen by numerous authors, repeating not just what has been said before in the document but also repeating *how* it has been said in a style akin to that of many other essays (a sort of "meta" repetition).
- Although it is true that all things must come to an end, to end with repetition can put an abrupt and unwelcome brake on all the momentum of the main idea that has been gathering steadily in the previous paragraphs.

The challenge, then, is to try to end a document without suddenly stalling or going against the forward movement you've generated. To do this, the emphasis could be more than just peering at what might be some next steps in research or inquiry. Instead, if the main idea has been discussed thoroughly enough, the writer could choose to end the message by bringing the audience to look ahead from a new perspective.

This may not always be easy or even feel feasible for writers who may be very tired or just eager to put their work behind them as they finish their assignment. But following the standard formula for concluding an essay can also make a writer seem a little less thoughtful and interesting because their conclusion will feel very (perhaps too) familiar. Leaving the reader with something substantial to think about at the end of an essay is a more effective way to convey confidence and mastery of a topic.

Part III: Conclusions That Look Forward, Not Backward— Some Examples

There are, of course, reasonable motives to repeat or summarize information that was previously discussed in a document. This is often done in teaching materials in which the first goal is to help students learn important aspects of a certain discipline. This can be helpful for students to solidify their understanding of a new or complex topic.

Even this book summarizes each chapter with a section that highlights its major points. But the intention of these sections is not focused on having readers only "review" the content in a chapter right after reading it; instead, their main function is to help students "apply" the suggestions of each chapter by creating a summary that takes the form of a series of gentle commands or directions. These sections can act also act as a memory trigger, reminding students of arguments in the book that they might have read six weeks or six months in the past. As a result, these "review and apply" endings are more like tools that can be used to facilitate future action rather than to simply review previous reading.

Good speeches often provide interesting examples of arguments that close without repetition. In 1962, John F. Kennedy made a speech at Rice University that aimed to persuade the nation that sending men to the moon was a useful and realizable goal. After opening with the claim that there seemed to be an increase in important questions in modern life that needed to be answered, Kennedy depicted rocket travel to the moon as a means to start answering those questions. The end of the speech offered a glimpse at what could be achieved *after* facing those questions:

> Many years ago, the great British explorer George Mallory, who was to die on Mount Everest, was asked why did he want to climb it. He said, "Because it is there."
>
> Well, space is there, and we're going to climb it, and the moon and the planets are there, *and new hopes for knowledge and peace are there* [emphasis added]. And, therefore, as we set sail, we ask God's blessing on the most hazardous and dangerous and greatest adventure on which man has ever embarked.*

Another kind of "call to action" is often found in the conclusions of academic review articles. Although not as passionate and

---

* John F. Kennedy, "Address at Rice University on the Nation's Space Effort," speech given at Rice University, September 12, 1962, archived at "Historic Speeches" webpage of the John F. Kennedy Presidential Library website, accessed January 6, 2023, https://www.jfklibrary.org /learn/about-jfk/historic-speeches/address-at-rice-university-on-the-nations-space-effort.

eloquent as the speech by Kennedy, these review articles display a similar a sense of excitement about making new discoveries or doing important new things. One typical example (among thousands of extant articles) is a piece called "Sleep problems in childhood psychiatric disorders—a review of the latest science."* The authors end the article noting the growth of research studies in this topic but are careful to note five areas of particular importance, including "the measurement of sleep" and "treatment studies," especially "well-designed randomized controlled trials (RCTs)." They then wrap up this concluding section by trying to evoke the vast amount of work to be done in the future—a measure not only of the potential of well-targeted studies ahead but also of the urgency to make up for lost time: "We hope we have justified why it is fruitful to learn more about sleep in children and adolescents suffering from other disorders—and we believe this knowledge has clinical value. . . . Since the days of Hippocrates, the value of sleep for good health has been discussed (see Suchecki et al., 2012)—but perhaps only now are paediatric researchers really waking up to this."

The growing desire for authors to end their books with a call to action has inspired some creative variations in the standard version of conclusions. For instance, the afterword section of a book has been changed, in some cases, from a reflection piece written by a person other than the author to a venue giving freer rein to writers to reflect on their own work. Surgeon and writer Atul Gawande does this in his 2007 memoir about working in the medical profession, *Better*. In this new kind of afterword (which seems more like

---

* Alice M. Gregory and Avi Sadeh, "Annual research review: Sleep problems in childhood psychiatric disorders—a review of the latest science," *Journal of Child Psychology and Psychiatry* 57, no. 3 (2016): 296–317.

a beginning than an ending), Gawande tries to answer a question that nags him at the end of the book: How does one physician among millions of health care professionals really make an impact? "I came up with five [answers to this question]," Guwande continues, "five suggestions for how one might make a worthy difference, for how one might become, in other words, a positive deviant."* A similar example can be found in the concluding chapter of the 2022 book *Sustainability: A History*.† The author "ends with a discussion of 10 challenges faced by the sustainability movement." Appropriately, this last chapter is titled "The Future."‡

I tend to favor the conclusions that lean toward the future because looking ahead implies cultivating a point of view that is not self-satisfied or complacent. It implicitly acknowledges that new problems and new challenges will always face us. They will never end. Even if some old problems are wrapped up nicely or manage to fade away, new ones always arise. While we shouldn't become paranoid about the inevitability of problems and challenges facing

---

* Atul Gawande, *Better: A Surgeon's Notes on Performance* (New York: Picador, 2007), 250.

† Jeremey L. Caradonna, *Sustainability: A History: Revised and Updated Edition* (Oxford: Oxford University Press, 2022).

‡ Ibid., 237. In works ending with a "to do" list, one can notice a cross-fertilization of writing genres. The end of *Sustainability* looks very much like the listicle about buying cheap airline tickets online that was cited in this book's introduction. While the listicle genre has existed for centuries, the word "listicle" and especially its wide use on the internet is much more recent. Its current popularity may be due to the promise of being able to unearth nuggets of actionable wisdom without being required to work through the complicated arguments within a book. (In order to be able to skip these detailed proofs, authors of listicles should have strong reputations in their domain, which is key to gaining their readers' trust in the absence of detailed arguments.) So, while the listicle may have its roots in printed documents, its wider recent use is probably due to its success in blogs and related articles on the internet.

us as individuals or as communities, we should remain vigilant. To do that, we need to keep alert and keep learning.

While an individual subject may have an ending of some sort, we need to apply our intelligence to new and emerging problems—problems that we don't or can't see today. Encouraging our minds to look toward tomorrow by building upon what we've learned from the past is one way to accomplish that.

Conclusion: Maintain Momentum Until the Very End

In some ways, writing *and* reading any kind of document is like climbing a hill or mountain—a steady progression through evidence and argument toward a higher understanding of a topic. (Of course, some mountains are higher and steeper than others.) While the effort and excitement of getting to the top of that hill is rewarding, the truly enticing achievement of climbing that hill is the ability to see a world beyond. The end of a written piece can accomplish a similar thing: it can suggest to the reader that more can be discovered now that we (the writer and reader) have journeyed together to reach a new plateau of understanding. In other words, the conclusion discusses an idea that is closely related to the essay or paper we've just finished that might itself become the topic of *another* piece. If done successfully, this ending could demonstrate to the reader that the writer is working, thinking, and sharing insights in a document all the way to the last word. From a reader's perspective, that can be an attractive and energetic way to culminate an intellectual journey and even begin a new one.

Review and Apply: Conclusions

- Most conclusions aim to remind the reader of a piece's main points and may also add an intriguing question or extra insight to spice up the ending.
- Merely repeating points made earlier in a document abruptly goes against the forward momentum of most good writing, which features ideas building upon one another to show or prove something.
- If you've been successful in terms of form, content, and alignment of ideas to support a main theme, it may not be at all necessary to remind the reader of the preceding argument as a way to wrap up a piece.
- Continue the forward momentum of your work by beginning to describe the *next* big idea that can now be seen differently or more clearly thanks to your writing.

Conclusion

Using "One Idea" to Navigate a World in Flux

∙∙

The one-idea rule was conceived, in part, as a response to a phenomenon I saw among some students that often broke my heart: a fear of expressing their own ideas. I had trained to become a university professor for many reasons, mostly because of my desire to share my enthusiasm about the study of history. But that enthusiasm came from a deeper personal tendency—a love of learning and an excitement in discovering new insights about the world around me. Being an extrovert, I naturally wanted to share the delight of some of my discoveries with others. While not everybody is an extrovert, most everybody has ideas about the world around them that they think are important for others to understand. How frustrating and discouraging it must be, then, to feel reluctant and even fearful to express important personal truths for fear of being contradicted . . . or even wrong.

Observing this fear among some of my students broke my heart because being "wrong" is usually just a normal step people take toward acquiring new skills and knowledge. When any person begins to learn about a new domain, they are almost always wrong about something. If one becomes fearful of making mistakes or being wrong, that can translate, in some extreme cases, into a fear of learning. How tragic, when learning is one of the greatest joys a person can experience! If a student fears or even loathes some aspects of learning (i.e., being in a classroom and going to school), then some elements of teaching as experienced by that student must have been poorly conceived and/or executed.

Having witnessed this trend early in my teaching career, I started to notice popular pedagogical tools that might contribute to that fear. Many influential books on writing (which might vary in format, from dry textbooks to more passionate style guides) seemed built to instill fear into readers who dare put pen to paper. Instead of being focused on *how* to write, many instructors of writing have been focused (for many years) on how *not* to write, assigning students to read books filled with warnings and admonitions such as the hugely influential phrase made popular in 1959, "omit needless words."*

These kinds of directives, often barked out in brief commands more appropriate to a military drill sergeant, are not only intimidating; they also are very much "out of order." While writers who are young or lack confidence certainly need to learn the basics of writing good sentences so they can be understood, they are more in

---

* This is a directive from the very popular writing style guide (and de facto primer and textbook for millions of Americans), now in its fourth edition, called *The Elements of Style*, which is often referenced by the last names of the authors: Strunk and White. See William Strunk Jr. and E. B. White, *The Elements of Style*, 4th ed. (New York: Pearson, 1999). While Strunk published the first edition in 1920, E. B. White greatly expanded this guide in 1959. It was at that time that the book's popularity skyrocketed, doubtlessly buoyed by White's reputation as the premier editor for the *New Yorker*.

need of writing practice that allows them to enjoy writing through finding their own voice. An apt analogy would be the predicament of a person taking voice lessons who has not sung much before. If the first voice lesson begins with "You're singing off key" or "Your voice is too loud," almost any beginning student would feel like their efforts are unattractive, off target, and unappreciated.

In contrast, the pedagogical approach of the one-idea rule insists that the first step in learning how to write is to write. The one-idea rule is designed to be a light load for writers to bear on their shoulders, giving them enough grounding to reduce their mistakes and keep their balance but not an enormous amount of material that might weigh them down.

So, if the one-idea rule does succeed in giving writers confidence today about expressing their own ideas, what could be the long-term benefits of using the rule tomorrow? For individual writers, gaining well-deserved confidence to express ideas will have the obvious advantage of promoting their work and opinions with clarity, which will almost always have a positive impact on their lives and careers. The one-idea rule may be especially helpful when writers encounter domains and controversies that are highly charged and full of confusing or unreliable information. Examining debates through the lens of the one-idea rule can reveal which arguments seem to have some merit (supported by evidence and logical thinking) and which don't.

There is an added benefit to being better able to discern and create arguments about meaningful topics. As times become more complicated, it becomes more important that people express themselves clearly so they can contribute their understanding of complex issues when it is needed. And making sure multiple voices can be heard clearly is necessary because no one person can provide a robust understanding of any topic (including writing) without listening to the viewpoints of others. Understanding the problems and opportunities we face today requires that people compare and contrast their respective versions of the world. Often, what we know about contemporary life is a mosaic created as a "group project" where the parameters can expand in proportion to the scale of the problem—from creating a report with a classmate on the latest trends in nutrition to scientists working around the world on ways to prevent and cure cancer.

In the search for truth, conclusions are sometimes less important than the reasoning used to arrive at those conclusions. That's because exposing that reasoning can implicitly solicit others to join in the ongoing search for truth (through offering critiques and new information). The one-idea rule constantly reminds writers to "show their work" to others in the documents they produce. If your contributions help others create better insights (through better evidence or reasoning), then even your mistakes can be seen as helping to improve the world.

The one-idea rule can become a steady companion that will help you to trust in your abilities to contribute valuable ideas to important matters at school, at work, and in your communities. In a world in which rapid changes require constant recalibration between what we used to understand and the new realities that we face, the one-idea rule will help you articulate what you do know as well as identify and better describe what you don't know. Building on this awareness, people can more efficiently seek out new sources and experts to help improve their appreciation of emerging issues. And by learning from each other in this way, we will become better equipped to solve challenging problems.

Acknowledgments

· ·

Teaching and writing have been two of the greatest joys of my career, and this book has given me the opportunity to deepen my experience in both domains. For that, I'm grateful to my publisher, Matt Holt, and my editor, Katie Dickman, for supporting this "one idea" that may help more people with their writing than I could ever hope to teach in person. (Thanks, too, to my colleague Rich Gravelin for introducing me to Matt Holt!)

Teachers have had a huge impact on my personal development, and many of them have inspired important aspects of *The One-Idea Rule*. My eleventh-grade high school English instructor at Coral Gables High, Jenny Krugman, played a particularly important role in my education, and I have deliberately used her as a model for the "teaching style" of this book. She was devoted to the intellectual development of *all* her students. In her classroom, she began this process by using classic literature to introduce ideas whose complexity had not yet been imagined by most sixteen-year-olds. While writing about these new ideas could be intimidating, Mrs. Krugman's students also knew that she would always be available to help navigate these beautiful but deep waters. In fact, as she showed us through engaging lectures and discussions, the depth of these ideas often turned out to be the source of their greatest beauty. This realization encouraged young minds to see complicated or difficult concepts as sources of fascination whose intriguing secrets could be comprehended if we used the right tools to open them up. In sum, she respected students and their potential; we loved her for that.

Other teachers who have made a similar mark on me and this book include: Mrs. Cervantes, Mrs. Bernabei, and Mr. Chingrine at Silver Bluff Elementary School; Mr. Lemon, Mrs. Burns, and Mrs. Ketchum at the Dade County gifted program for elementary students; Mr. Hernandez ("Mr. H") and Ellen Kempler at Shenandoah Junior High; Geoffrey Freer, Peggy Hall, Jacqueline Esco, and Bill Ledue (our incredible band director) at Coral Gables; Robert Doran, Barry O'Connell, and Robert Gross at Amherst College (and thanks, Bob, for those masterful and motivating critiques of my freshman papers); Audley Webster at the University of Miami; and, finally, Morton Keller, Jackie Jones, and James Kloppenberg at Brandeis University.

New ideas need nurturing, and for that I had some friends and colleagues who were patient enough to accompany me during various parts of my latest intellectual venture. In many walks between Belmont and Arlington, Massachusetts, Immaculata De Vivo offered an ear as well as very sound responses to my ever-in-progress work. Colleagues from Harvard Business Publishing—Kevin Russell, Van Morrill, Natalie Blanchette, Seldron Geziben, Ashley Parker, and Lucy Swedberg—have indulged and/or supported my enthusiasm for this "one idea." My old workmate from HBP, George Stergios, provided invaluable feedback in the early stages of work on this manuscript and kept me from getting tripped up by the many "rabbit holes" related to this topic. HBR.org editor Paige

Cohen applied her editorial genius to the first published article (on HBR.org) about the one-idea rule. My colleagues involved with writing coaching at Harvard Business School have shared very kind wishes and interest, especially Sasha Watkins. (And I should note that my work with HBS students since 2018 convinced me of the potential utility of the one-idea rule for many kinds of writing.) My dear friend from Arlington, Olga Yulikova, also became a very helpful cheerleader for the project in its later stages, which was so needed on those days when my energy was flagging.

My sister, Cecilia Rennella Carter, is a great editor. I took advantage of my privileged position as her brother to bug her repeatedly for ideas and feedback when I really needed it. My parents, Cosme and Cherolyn Rennella, also offered their interest and enthusiasm for their son's latest project. Finally, my two sons (now twenty-one and eighteen years old) were obliged to play the role of "focus group," often fielding questions from me about their own writing issues or about certain ideas and passages from my book. In the process, I've used some material and insights from Davis (including the headshot used for this book!) and have cornered Ben in more conversations about *One-Idea* than he ever thought were necessary.

It was good to hear from Ben in the spring of 2022 that he often thought of the one-idea rule as he worked on assignments for high school. "Really?" I asked. "Well, it's helpful," he responded with a smile. Kids don't often go out of their way to flatter their parents, so I am most grateful for this reassurance!

–Mark Rennella
January 2023

Index

About the Author

....

M ark Rennella has given students and professionals helpful advice about writing throughout his career, most recently as a writing coach for MBA candidates at Harvard Business School. Mark earned a PhD in American history from Brandeis University and has taught literature and American history at Harvard University, the University of Miami, and the University of Tours (France). His publications include *Entrepreneurs, Managers, and Leaders: What the Airline Industry Can Teach Us About Leadership*, coauthored with Anthony J. Mayo and Nitin Nohria, former dean of Harvard Business School. Mark's books, articles, business case studies, and collaborative writing endeavors have garnered him critical praise from historians, academicians, and business leaders alike. His concept of the "one-idea rule" was included among HBR.org's ten favorite management tips for 2022. He currently works as an editor for Harvard Business Publishing.